The life of General Hugh Mercer

John T. Goolrick

Alpha Editions

This edition published in 2019

ISBN : 9789353600969

Design and Setting By
Alpha Editions
email - alphaedis@gmail.com

THE LIFE OF
GENERAL HUGH MERCER

Hugh Mercer

THE LIFE

OF

GENERAL HUGH MERCER

With brief sketches of General George Washington, John Paul Jones, General George Weedon, James Monroe and Mrs. Mary Ball Washington, who were friends and associates of General Mercer at Fredericksburg; also a sketch of Lodge No. 4, A. F. and A. M., of which Generals Washington and Mercer were members; and a genealogical table of the Mercer family.

BY

JOHN T. GOOLRICK

Illustrated

New York & Washington
THE NEALE PUBLISHING COMPANY
1906

Copyright, 1906, By
JOHN T. GOOLRICK

ILLUSTRATIONS

THIS book is affectionately dedicated to my wife, a great-granddaughter of George Mason, who was an intimate friend and associate of General Hugh Mercer.

INTRODUCTION

An introduction is only necessary to this Life of Mercer in order to return thanks to others for what I have herein obtained from them, as well as to disclaim any very marked originality for some things herein written. For instance, I could not and do not claim any great originality for the brief description of the battles of Culloden or of Princeton. Both have been described so often and by so many writers, that there is "nothing new under the sun" to be said about them. I only introduce them here that I may give a full and complete history of the life of Mercer; without them I could not have done so. I return thanks and acknowledge myself under obligations to James D. Law, Esq., of Germantown, Pa.; Rev. J. Lindsay Patton, Ashland, Va.; Judge Beverly R. Wellford, Richmond, Va., and Corbin W. Mercer, Esq., Richmond, Va., for some things that I have embodied in this small volume, and which appear with quotation marks.

I was constrained to write of General Hugh Mercer because I thought that such a life as he lived, and such a death as he died, should be written about; and should be written about by some one who is identified with Fredericksburg, the home of Mercer. How perfectly or imperfectly I have performed the task which I have voluntarily undertaken, I submit to the charitable criticism of my readers.

Respectfully,
JOHN T. GOOLRICK.

Fredericksburg, Va., March 1, 1906.

CHAPTER I

THE Highlands of Scotland, land of brown heath and shaggy wood—"land of the mountain and the flood"—has always been celebrated in song and story. Its stern and wild mountains, its dark and silent glens, its deep-lying lochs beneath the shadow of the hills, its silent, whirling mists and sudden storms, are the scenes of strange romance and ghastly tragedy. It is a very playground for the novelist's excited imagination and the poet's wildest fancy. But withal, so barren in soil and harsh in climate, that the inhabitants of the Highlands early gave themselves up to the delights of the chase, or the dangers of the sea, the pursuit of arms, or the joy of battle.

Picturesque in costume, splendid in muscular development, trained in the use of arms, proud of their race, loyal to their clan, they boasted their fidelity to their friends, and that they never turned their backs to a foe. Restless, inclined to travel, quick to adapt themselves to new surround-

11

ings, the Highlanders of Scotland sought their fortunes abroad, rising to fame and wealth in many a Continental country, becoming the leaders in trade and commerce, in Colonial enterprise and in war, in all parts of the Northern Hemisphere. Frugal, industrious, persevering and brave, success rewarded their undertakings. Characterised beyond all else by loyalty to their King, they were the most devoted of the adherents of the ill-fated house of Stuart, and they gathered around that fatal standard with romantic devotion. To their loyalty this land is indebted for not a few of its best citizens and noblest heroes. The land of the Highlanders—Bonnie Scotland —has given to the world in all departments of life, great men who have taken conspicuous parts in its history in war and peace. The men from the land of Bobby Burns have made their impress on the age and on the people among whom they have lived, and none occupies a higher niche in its Hall of Fame than General Hugh Mercer.

Hugh Mercer was born in Aberdeen, Scotland, in the year 1725. He descended on his paternal side from a long line of ministers of the Church of Scotland. The Rev. William Mercer, his father, was in charge of the Manse at Pittsligo, Aberdeenshire, from 1720 to 1748, and although some biographers of Mercer give the date of his birth as 1721, the records of this church show that he was baptised in 1726; it is therefore thought now, that more accurate history should place his birth in the year 1725. On his mother's side he was closely related to the Munro family; her name being Anna Munro, daughter of Sir Robert Munro, who fought with conspicuous distinction in the British Army at Fontenoy, on the Continent, and elsewhere; and who, ordered home to oppose the young Pretender, was killed in 1746 while commanding British troops at the Battle of Falkirk.

Mercer matriculated in the School of Medicine of Marschall College in the year 1740, graduating in the year 1744. He had hardly commenced the practice of his profession ere Prince Charlie made his "dash for a throne" which startled and, for a while, stupefied the British by its daring and brilliancy, but which was very ephemeral in its existence. The Scotch, especially those from the Highlands, were always loyal to the House of Stuart, and "Wha shall be King but Charlie?" as it was played on the bagpipes by the kilted Highlanders, his admiration for the people whom the Pretender represented, and his

convictions of the justice of his cause,
stirred up the martial and patriotic spirit
of Hugh Mercer, who joined Charles Edward's Army as an Assistant Surgeon.
History and tradition are both silent as to
when Mercer "linked his fortune and his
fate" to the cause of the Pretender.
Whether he was on the fatal field of Falkirk on January 17, 1746, we have no record; but on April 16, 1746, at Culloden,
near Inverness, he is found in the army of
Prince Charles. The Duke of Cumberland
was on that day in command of the Royal
forces against the Highlanders, and when
the sun went down on the field of carnage,
Mercer shared with his chieftain the gloom
of his defeat—a defeat that marked the end
of the ambition of the Pretender and the
hopes of the Stuarts. The victorious shouts
of the army of the Duke sounded a veritable
dirge to a cause that was then irrevocably
lost. The last grand stand had been made,
and all was over.

Sir Walter Scott, with his splendid
genius for picturing and portraying, in the
"Tales of a Grandfather," gives a graphic
account of the Battle of Culloden; an extract from which may not be inappropriate
to embody in this sketch. After narrating
the events of importance that led up to the

battle, the marching and the counter-
marching of the armies of Prince Charles
and the Duke of Cumberland, and especially the unsuccessful night attack on April
15th by the Army of the Pretender, Sir
Walter Scott wrote:

"As the lines approached each other the
artillery opened their fire by which the
Duke of Cumberland's army suffered very
little and that of the Highlanders a great
deal, for the English guns being well served
made lanes through the ranks of the enemy,
while the French artillery scarcely killed a
man. To remain steady and inactive under
this galling fire would have been a trial to
the best-disciplined troops, and it is no
wonder that the Highlanders showed great
impatience under an annoyance peculiarly
irksome to their character; some threw
themselves down to escape the artillery,
some called out to advance, and a few broke
their ranks and fled.

"The cannonade lasted for about an
hour; at length the Clans became so impa-
tient that Lord George Murray was about
to give the order to advance, when the
Highlanders from the centre and right
wings rushed, without orders, furiously
down, after their usual manner of attack-
ing, sword in hand, being received with

heavy fire both of cannon and grape-shot.
They became so confused that they got hud-
dled together in their onset, without any
distinction of Clans or regiments. Not-
withstanding this disorder, the fury of
their charge broke through Munro's and
Burrel's regiments, which formed the left
of the Duke of Cumberland's line; but that
General had anticipated the possibility of
such an event, and had strengthened his
second line so as to form a steady support
in case any part of his first should give
way. The Highlanders, partially victorious, continued to advance with fury, and although much disordered and partly disarmed (having thrown away their guns
on the very first charge), they rushed on
Sempill's Regiment, in the second line, with
unabated fury. That steady corps was
drawn up three deep, the first rank kneel-
ing, and the third standing upright. They
reserved their fire until the fugitives of
Burrel's and Munro's broken regiments
had escaped round the flanks and through
the intervals of the second line. By this
time the Highlanders were within a yard of
the bayonet point, when Sempill's battalion
poured in their fire with so much accuracy
that it brought down a great many of the
assailants, and forced the rest to turn back.

A few pressed on, but unable to break through Sempill's Regiment were bayoneted by the first rank. The attack of the Highlanders was the less efficient that on this occasion most of them had laid aside their targets, expecting a march rather than a battle.

"While the right of the Highland line sustained their national character, though not with their usual success, the MacDonnalds on the left seemed uncertain whether they would attack or not. It was in vain Lord George Murray called out to them, 'Claymore,' telling the murmurers of this haughty tribe 'that if they behaved with their usual valor they would convert the left into the right and that he would in future call himself MacDonnald.' It was equally in vain that the gallant Keppoch charged with a few of his near relations, while his Clan, a thing before unheard of, remained stationary.

"The Chief was near the front of the enemy and was exclaiming, with feelings that cannot be appreciated, 'My God, have the children of my tribe forsaken me?' At that instant he received several shots, which closed his earthly account, leaving him only time to advise his favorite nephew to shift for himself.

"The three regiments of the MacDonnalds were by this time aware of the rout of their right wing, and retreated in good order upon the second line. A body of cavalry from the right of the King's army was commanded to attack them on their retreat, but was checked by a fire from the French pickets, who advanced to support the MacDonnalds. At the same moment another decisive advantage was gained by the Duke's army over the Highland right wing. A body of horse making six hundred cavalry, with three companies of Argyleshire Highlanders, had been detached to take possession of the Park walls; the three companies of infantry had pulled down the east wall of the inclosure and put to the sword about a hundred of the insurgents to whom its defense had been assigned. They then demolished the western wall, which permitted the dragoons, by whom they were accompanied, to ride through the inclosure and get out upon the open moor to the westward, and form so as to threaten the rear and flank of the Prince's second line.

"Gordon of Abbachie, with his Lowland Aberdeenshire regiment, was ordered to fire upon these cavalry, which he did with some effect. The Campbells then lined the north wall of the inclosure and commenced

a fire upon the right flank of the Highlanders' second line. That line, increased by
the MacDonnalds, who retired upon it, still
showed a great number of men keeping
their ground, many of whom had not fired a
shot. Lord Elcho rode up to the Prince and
eagerly exhorted him to put himself at the
head of those troops who yet remained and
make a last exertion to recover the day and
at least die like one worthy of having contended for a crown."

But all this was too late—the Pretender
had been defeated; and his army, broken
and shattered, fled from the field, hotly pursued by the Duke of Cumberland and his
army. Of the treatment of the fallen and
their allies, Sir Walter Scott thus writes:
"The soldiers had orders to exercise to-
wards the unfortunate natives the utmost
extremities of war; they shot, therefore,
the male inhabitants who fled at their ap-
proach; they plundered the houses of the
chieftains; they burnt the cabins of the
peasants; they were guilty of every out-
rage against women, old age, and infancy,
and where the soldiers fell short of these
extremities it was their own mildness of
temper or that of some officer of gentler
mood which restrained the license of their
hand."

And in conclusion, in his discussion of this battle, its causes and its results, Sir Walter Scott wrote: "Looking at the whole in a general point of view, there can be no doubt that it presents a dazzling picture to the imagination, being a romance of real life, equal in splendour and interest to any which could be devised by fiction. A primitive people, residing in a remote quarter of the empire and themselves but a small portion of the Scottish Highlanders, fearlessly attempted to place the British Crown on the head of the last scion of those ancient kings whose descent was traced to their own mountains.

"This gigantic task they undertook in favor of a youth of twenty-one, who landed on their shore without support of any kind and threw himself on their generosity. They assembled an army in his behalf with men unaccustomed to arms, the amount of the most efficient part of which never exceeded two thousand; they defeated two disciplined armies commanded by officers of experience and reputation, penetrated deep into England, approached within ninety miles of the capital, made the Crown tremble on the King's head, and were only suppressed by concurrent disadvantages which it was impossible for human nature to surmount. It is, therefore, natural that this civil strife should have been long the chosen theme of the poet, the musician, and the novelist.''

In his flight, the Pretender was like a hare hunted by hounds. Flora MacDonnald, a Scottish maiden, foiled his pursuers; and at length he reached France in safety. His loyal and loving followers found refuge in any way possible, hunted down, mercilessly butchered when caught. The terrible tragedy of the battle was as nothing compared to the butchery of these fugitives by the relentless and implacable Duke of Cumberland. Historians may differ as to the right and righteousness of the cause of Prince Charles Edward. None can deny that William, Duke of Cumberland, has rightly written his name as infamous by his treatment of the fallen foe. Campbell sweetly though sadly sang of Culloden:

Lochiel, Lochiel, beware of the day
When the Lowlands shall meet thee in
    battle array;
For a field of the dead rushes red on my
    sight,
And the Clans of Culloden are scattered in
    flight.

They rally, they bleed, for their kingdom
    and crown;
Woe, woe to the riders that trample them
    down.

For dark and despairing my sight I may
    seal,
But man cannot cover what God would
    reveal;
'Tis the sunset of life gives me mystical
    lore,
And coming events cast their shadows
    before.
I tell thee, Culloden's dread echoes shall
    ring
With the bloodhounds that bark for their
    fugitive king.

CHAPTER II

HAVING, as has been before stated, fallen
under the shadow of a great sorrow by the
disastrous ending of the Battle of Culloden,
and having eluded the vigilance of the min-
ions of the "Bloody Butcher," Dr. Hugh
Mercer, in the fall of the year 1746, embarked at Leith for America, landing a few
weeks thereafter at Philadelphia. He did
not remain long, however, in that city, but
made his home on the western borders of
the State of Pennsylvania, near what was
then known as Greencastle, now Mercersburg. And for some years he practised his
profession as a physician and, what was
customary in those days, as an apothecary.
In that then sparsely settled section, the
territory over which he rode, dispensing
calomel and using the lancet, was very
large. Among the varied experiences of
this eventful and heroic life, none proved
more helpful and beneficial than the ardu-
ous, unselfish years spent as a country doctor in Colonial times on the frontier of civi-
lisation in Pennsylvania, a profession for

which he was well fitted by education and training, and by the high qualities of endurance, patience, skill and courage. For the country doctor's life of that day needed all the strength of body and of brain, the steadfast will and tireless energy. It was a wild and busy life in an unsettled region of scattered homes; distance and danger were daily encountered, for the Indians still hovered upon the frontier, and life and liberty were often imperiled by their unexpected attacks.

To this strange chance of fate and fortune came the soldier-surgeon of Culloden, and here he lived and labored for many years, amid privation and peril, dauntless and devoted; friend, healer, counsellor, benefactor to all within the circle of his far-reaching ministry of comfort and cure —the country doctor of the past. How shall we picture a life, a man, so worthy of reproduction and remembrance?

"God gives to every man
 The virtue, temper, understanding, taste,
 That lifts him into life, and lets him fall
 Just in the niche he has ordained to fill."

Known to all the inhabitants of the region round about, loved and welcomed everywhere, believed in and looked up to as one who not only healed the sick, but one who strengthened the weak, comforted the weary, and cheered the sorrowing, Hugh Mercer's life as a country doctor day by day in active duty, with saddle-bags filled with remedies for human ills, the old-fashioned medicines and the ever-ready lancet for bloodletting, was a splendid preparation for the hardships and privations he was in the future called upon to endure. A life of hardship ennobled by duty well done, and consecrated by self-sacrifice.

It was a rough school, but a thorough one, in which the country doctor learned the lessons of life. As he rode amid the forest solitudes, vigilant, alert, or visited the waiting homes to which his presence brought succor and relief, his memories of the past merged in duties of the present, with only faith and fortitude as guides upon the way, his life might have seemed unsatisfying to a nature less hopeful, less heroic. All honor to this man, and the many like him, whose daily round of sympathetic toil is brightened by the approval of his conscience and the benedictions of suffering humanity. The country doctor's lasting monument lives in the hearts that loved and reverenced him; and no higher tribute to his memory can be written than the tender and inspiring words of heavenly recognition and reward, "I was sick and ye visited me."

It was a history-making era, that of the year of 1755—the time of Braddock's disastrous defeat by the French and Indians, in his attempt to capture Fort Duquesne. There and then George Washington's splendid career began, and there Mercer made his first public and prominent appearance as a Captain in the ill-fated army of Braddock, conspicuous for his bravery on the memorable July 9, 1755, of which has been said, "The Continentals gave the only glory to that humiliating disaster." "History," says another, "furnishes few pages so replete with instances of official incompetence and consequent failure as that expedition, yet in the list of its Colonial heroes, the name of Hugh Mercer stands ever bright." In this engagement, Mercer was severely wounded; and, having been left behind by his own army in its panic-stricken flight, after a perilous tramp through a trackless wild, he at length rejoined his comrades and again commenced the work of healing the sick at his old locality.

The Indians with their French allies be-

Hugh Mercer as a Country Doctor in Pennsylvania

OPPOSITE P. 26

coming very aggressive and warlike, its residents for self-protection formed themselves into military associations of which Colonel Armstrong was made Commander. In one of these companies Hugh Mercer was made Captain. His commission as such is dated March, 1756, and he was given the supervision of a very large territory, with Bridgeport (then called McDowell's Fort) as his headquarters.

During all this time he practised as a physician among the people and as surgeon to the garrison. In one of these Indian fights he was again wounded and abandoned to his foes. "Closely pursued by his savage foes," says a very interesting historian, "he providentially found a place of safety in the hollow trunk of a tree, around which the Indians rested and discussed the prospect of scalping him in the near future. When they had taken their departure, he took out in another direction and completely outwitted them." Sick with his wounds and worn out with his recent struggles, he began a lonely march of over a hundred miles through an unbroken forest. To sustain existence, he was compelled to live on roots and herbs, the carcass of a rattlesnake proving his most nourishing and palatable meal. He finally succeeded in re-

joining his command at Fort Cumberland.
He was in command of one of the companies which captured an Indian settle-
ment at Kittanning in 1756, but was again
wounded. In recognition and appreciation
of his services, sacrifices and sufferings in
these Indian wars, as well as his deeds of
daring, the Corporation of Philadelphia
presented him with a note of thanks and a
splendid memorial medal.

Mercer was placed in command of the
garrison at Shippensburg in the summer of
1757, and was promoted to the rank of Major in December of that year, and placed in
command of the forces of the province of
Pennsylvania west of the Susquehanna. In
that year, 1758, he was in command of a
part of the expedition of General Forbes
against Fort Duquesne. Whether Hugh
Mercer met George Washington at Braddock's defeat, or at the headquarters of the
Forbes expedition against Fort Duquesne,
there seems to be some conflict of opinion
and statement among his biographers. The
time and place of that meeting is of no very
material moment. One thing seems to be
absolutely certain, that they did meet, and
an attachment sprang up between them
which lasted as long as Mercer lived. And,
further, that as a result of that meeting and

that attachment, on the advice and at the suggestion of Washington, Virginia became the home of Hugh Mercer, and the State of Pennsylvania lost him as a citizen.

CHAPTER III

SOME TIME after the end of the French-Indian wars on the western borders of Pennsylvania, Hugh Mercer moved to Fredericksburg, Virginia; and during his residence in that town another Scotchman lived there, a fellow-citizen, one whose name was destined to "go down the ages, sung by poets and sages"—John Paul Jones! John Paul had only one home in America, and that was Fredericksburg. There his brother, William Paul, lived and died. There he lies buried. It was while John Paul was in Fredericksburg that he added Jones to his name, and from there he went forth as a Lieutenant of the Continental Navy. These two illustrious Scotchmen, Hugh Mercer and John Paul Jones, no doubt often met and talked of the land of their birth beyond the seas. Both, however, became illustrious in the cause of the Colonies in their struggle to be free from the domination of Great Britain, even though Scotland was one of its constituent territories. In Fredericksburg,

Mercer commenced the practice of his profession as a physician, his residence for a number of years being a two-story frame house on the corner of Princess Ann and Amelia streets. His office and apothecary shop was located in the building now standing at the corner of Main and Amelia streets.

An English traveller in 1784 published an account of a visit that he had made to Fredericksburg during the Revolution, and made this statement:

"I arrived in Fredericksburg and put up at an inn kept by one Weedon, who is now a general officer in the American Army, and who was then very active and zealous in blowing the flames of sedition. In Fredericksburg, I called upon a worthy and intimate friend, Dr. Hugh Mercer, a physician of great eminence and merit, and, as a man, possessed of almost every virtue and accomplishment. Dr. Mercer was afterwards Brigadier-General in the American Army, to accept of which appointment I have reason to believe he was greatly influenced by General Washington, with whom he had been long in intimacy and bonds of friendship. For Dr. Mercer was generally of a just and moderate way of thinking and possessed of liberal sentiments and a generosity of principle very uncommon among those with whom he embarked.''

The inn to which this traveller referred was ''The Rising Sun Tavern,'' now standing on upper Main Street; and Weedon, who he said was actively engaged in blowing the flames of sedition, was brother-in-law of Mercer. This intensely loyal son of Great Britain was evidently a great admirer of Hugh Mercer; while he characterised the so-called disloyal colonist as wanting in that generosity of principle with which Mercer, he said, was greatly endowed.

Life in the quiet town of Fredericksburg during these years was uneventful. Mercer pursued the even tenor of his way as a country doctor, always a welcome guest in the hospitable homes of its people; he attended the meetings of Lodge No. 4, A. F. & A. M., of which he and George Washington were members, and occasionally paid a visit to the future ''Father of his Country'' at Mount Vernon.

Some time in the spring of 1775, a horseman suddenly dashed up the quiet streets of his town with the startling news that Virginia's Royal Governor, Dunmore, at Williamsburg, the capital, had removed the Colonial store of gunpowder from the mag-

The Office and Apothecary Shop of Hugh Mercer, Fredericksburg, Virginia

azine to the British man-of-war Magdalen.
This tyrannical and aggressive act upon the
part of Dunmore only intensified the mut-
terings of discontent already existing in
the colony, and added fuel to the flames
that were already burning. Messengers
were at once dispatched to the adjoining
counties urging decisive action, and the
horsemen and footmen came pouring in. A
meeting was then called, and an organization perfected of which we have this
record:

"Election of officers of minutemen and
regulars for Caroline, Spotsylvania, King
George and Stafford counties, Virginia,
September 12, 1775. At a meeting of the
select committee for the district of this
county, the counties of Caroline, Stafford,
King George and Spotsylvania, the following officers were elected:

"Minutemen—Hugh Mercer, Colonel;
Mordecai Buckner, Lieutenant-Colonel;
Robert Johnson, Major.

"For Spotsylvania — L e w i s Willis,
George Stubblefield and Oliver Towles,
Captains; Robert Carter Page, Larkin
Chew, Francis Taliaferro, Lieutenants;
Henry Bartlett, Robert Dudley and Wins-
low Parker, Ensigns."

And "Mercer's Minutemen" commenced

the march to Williamsburg. Before proceeding very far, it is said that George Mason and others urged them to reconsider and wait for further and fuller information and not to act too hastily; and the cooler counsels of these advisers prevailed. Of this, Alexander Spotswood, in a letter to George Washington of date April 30, 1775, wrote:

"I am extremely glad to inform you that after a long debate it was agreed that we should not march to Williamsburg."

Four days later, George Washington set out from Mount Vernon for the Continental Congress. The abandonment of the undertaking may have been brought about by the want of ammunition, as Mercer wrote to Washington on April 25, 1775:

"We are not sufficiently supplied with powder; it may be proper to request of the gentlemen who join us from Fairfax and Prince William to come provided with an over-proportion of that article."

Returning to the town, they appointed a Committee of Safety and adopted a set of resolutions in which they pledged their sacred honor to resist all attempts against their rights and liberties, from whatever quarter they might be assailed, and agreed to be in readiness to defend the laws, the liberties and the rights of this or any sister colony from unjust and wicked invasion by force of arms, concluding with, "God save the liberties of America." It is claimed that this Declaration is prior in time to that of Mecklenburg, North Carolina, as it is to that of the Continental Congress at Philadelphia.

A thoughtful writer defines history as "philosophy teaching by example." If this be so, historic Fredericksburg ranks high in the rôle of great names and great deeds. Of the men who made our history in Colonial days, before and during the Revolutionary War, many were identified with that old town, visited there, met together in friendly converse or earnest counsel, and discussed the grave questions of the hour—England's oppressive measures and the resistance of the Colonies, the rights involved, the liberties invaded, and the crisis inevitable. George Washington was often there; Fredericksburg was the home of his mother. Hugh Mercer lived there as a physician; James Monroe, lawyer (who later led the advance of the Americans in the battle of Trenton and afterwards became President), also resided there; John Marshall, afterward Chief Justice, and George Mason of Gunston Hall,

leaders of thought, patriots of action, all
found Fredericksburg a pleasant and con-
venient meeting place in those days, omi-
nous of threatening strife and deadly conflict.

In September, 1774, the General Congress of the Colonies met in Philadelphia,
the assembled delegates representing the
best and wisest, the most determined and
patriotic men of the land. Peyton Randolph, of Virginia, was chosen president;
and a declaration of rights and a series of
resolutions were adopted which "for solid-
ity of reasoning, force of sagacity, and wis-
dom of conclusion" have never been ex-
celled. The session ended on the 26th of
October, and it was recommended that another Congress meet in May, 1775. The
war-cloud was lowering.

In March, 1775, the Virginia Convention
assembled in St. John's Church, Richmond,
and Patrick Henry's magnetic eloquence,
his splendid rallying cry of "Liberty or
death," stirred all hearts to decision and
action. During these months of hesitation,
anxiety, possible compromise, yet continued aggression, we can imagine this group
of patriots in Fredericksburg keenly alive
to the hazardous trend of public affairs
which culminated in open hostilities at Lex-

ington and Concord. The Rising Sun tavern was then the centre of public entertain-
ment; and its genial host was Mr. George
Weedon, who afterwards became a Major-
General in the Continental Army. The
cosy apartments of the inn, its bright wood
fires and comfortable surroundings, in-
duced good-fellowship and free exchange of
opinions. There was no need of argument,
as all were true patriots. It was surely as
picturesque a scene as history ever painted
—those men in conversation at the "Rising
Sun!" Washington, wise and calm; Mercer, with patriotic power and battle memories surging in his heart; impetuous Paul
Jones, eager for the fray; young Monroe,
summing up the wrongs of the Colonies,
and ready to avenge them; Marshall, the
learned jurist, the great advocate of justice, and George Mason, one of the great
lights of history, whose genius illuminated
the cause and established its principles.
Can we not see them all, great men, whose
example lives still, whose names are blaz-
oned on "the roll-call of the immortals."

Madam Washington, as she was called,
lived not far from the Rising Sun tavern,
and would have enjoyed the earnest dis-
cussions therein (which no doubt George
reported to her), as her sterling good sense

and keen observation made her opinions of decided weight and influence.

After the removal of the powder, above referred to, the news of unjustifiable acts of aggression by the Crown in other Colonies came thick and fast. Events with startling rapidity followed one after another. Concord and Lexington had been heard from; Virginia's Patrick Henry had uttered the words that were heard around the world; and the Revolution was inaugurated. Three regiments were formed. Henry was made Colonel of the First, elected over Hugh Mercer by one vote in a contest for the colonelcy.

William Woodford of Caroline County became Colonel of the Second, and Mercer, Colonel of the Third Regiment, of which his brother-in-law, Weedon, was the Lieutenant-Colonel; and Thomas Marshall of Fauquier County, the father of John Marshall who afterwards became Chief Justice, was the Major. About this time, Mercer, who had married Miss Isabella Gordon, daughter of John Gordon, resided in what is known as "The Sentry-Box," on lower Main Street, a house which is still in good condition and well preserved.

The election of Mercer to the colonelcy of this Third Regiment was a veritable case of the "office seeking the man," for when the storm-cloud of war first appeared, Mercer made an offer of his services to the Virginia Convention in these expressive but brief words: "Hugh Mercer will serve his adopted country and the cause of Liberty in any rank or station to which he may be assigned," words which found their echo in what he said later.

"We are not engaged," said he, "in a war of ambition, or I should not have been here. Every man should be content to serve in that station in which he can be most useful. For my part, I have but one object in view, and that is, the success of the cause; and God can witness how cheerfully I would lay down my life to secure it."

William Wirt, in his Life of Patrick Henry, has this to say in connection with Mercer's appointment:

"Three Regiments of one thousand men each was first determined on, and Patrick Henry's friends nominated him for Colonel of the First Regiment, it having been determined that this officer should be the Commander-in-Chief of the forces to be raised. The opposition united on Dr. Hugh Mercer of Fredericksburg, who had served with great distinction under Washington in the French and Indian War of 1755. It is no wonder that men, with so much at stake, should have hesitated to place in command of their entire forces a man of no military experience (Patrick Henry), however great his abilities as a civilian. The first ballot stood for Hugh Mercer 41, for Patrick Henry 40, for Thomas Nelson 8, and for William Woodford 1.

"The second ballot between the two highest resulted in the election of Mr. Henry, although Mercer and Woodford were officers of experience and ability. Nothing but the conviction of the majority that the qualities which made Mr. Henry a great political leader would also make him a good Colonel can explain their action in preferring him (Patrick Henry) as the Commander-in-Chief of the Virginia forces. Mercer was objected to for being a North Briton. In answer to this objection it was admitted that Mercer was born in Scotland, but that he came to America in his early years and had constantly resided in it from his first coming over; that his family and all his other connections were in this colony; that he had uniformly distinguished himself as a warm and firm friend of the rights of America; and what was a principal consideration, that he possessed great

military as well as literary abilities. Mr.
Nelson acknowledged Mercer's military
abilities, declared he would not oppose his
appointment, and hoped that he himself
would not be voted for. Mr. Woodford,
who was not at that time a member of the
Convention, spoke much in favor of Mercer, declaring that he was willing to serve
under him, as he knew him to be a fine
officer.''

Mercer's election is thus recorded in
the proceedings of the Virginia Convention:

''Wednesday, January 10, 1776, Convention proceeded by ballot to the appointment
of a Colonel of the Third Regiment, and
there was a majority of the whole Convention in favor of Hugh Mercer. Resolved,
therefore, that the said Hugh Mercer be
appointed Colonel of the Third Regiment.''

When the Committee of Safety heard of
Mercer's appointment, it passed these resolutions:

''The committee of the county, to express
their approbation of the appointment of
Col. Mercer, and to pay a tribute justly
due to the noble and patriotic conduct
which that gentleman has uniformly pursued since the commencement of our dis-
putes with the Mother Country, which was

so strikingly displayed on that occasion, entered into the following resolve:

"*Resolved*, That the thanks of this committee be presented to Colonel Hugh Mercer, Commander-in-Chief of the Battalion of Minute Men in the District of this County, and the counties of Caroline, Stafford, and King George; expressing the high sense of the importance of his appointment to that station, and our acknowledgements of his public spirit in sacrificing his private interest to the service of his Country.

"ALEXANDER DICK, Clerk."

And Colonel Mercer, at the head of his regiment, with his fife and drum, marched away from his adopted Virginia home, bidding good-by to his wife, children, and friends—"whom God ordained and the fates decreed" he should never, in this world, see again.

CHAPTER IV

COLONEL MERCER was ordered at once to report to Williamsburg—then the capital of Virginia—where there was a considerable encampment of troops. A writer in a very old periodical gives us an interesting account of Mercer while there, from which we quote:

"The commencement of the American Revolution found him in the midst of an extensive medical practice, surrounded by affectionate friends, and enjoying in the bosom of a happy family all the comforts of social life. Stimulated to action by a lofty spirit of patriotism, he broke from the endearments of domestic life, and gave to his country in that trying hour the energy and resources of a practiced and accomplished soldier. In 1775 he was in command of three regiments of minute men, and early in 1776 we find him zealously engaged, as Colonel of the Army of Virginia, in drilling and organizing the raw and ill-formed masses of men who, under the varied names

43

of sons of liberty, minutemen, volunteers, and levies, presented the bulk without the order, the mob without the discipline, of an army. To produce obedience and subordination among men who had entered into the war unpaid and unrestricted by command, was a severe and invidious task.

The courage, the fortitude, the self-possession of Colonel Mercer quailed not at these adverse circumstances, and, by the judicious exercise of mingled severity and kindness, he soon succeeded in reducing a mutinous soldiery to complete submission. Tradition has preserved the following anecdote, illustrating, in a striking manner, his characteristic promptitude and bravery:

Among the troops which arrived at Williamsburg, then the metropolis of Virginia, was a company of riflemen from beyond the mountains, commanded by Captain Gibson. A reckless insubordination and a violent opposition to military restraint had gained for this corps the sarcastic name of "Gibson's Lambs." They had not been long in camp before a mutiny arose among them, producing much excitement in the army, and alarming the inhabitants of the city. Freed from all command, they roamed

through the camp, threatening with instant
death any officer who would presume to exercise authority over them. In the height
of the rebellion an officer was dispatched
with the alarming tidings to the quarters
of Colonel Mercer. The citizens of the town
vainly implored him not to risk his life and
person amid this infuriated mob.

Reckless of personal safety, he instantly
repaired to the barracks of the mutinous
band, and directing a general parade of the
troops, he ordered Gibson's company to be
drawn up as offenders and violators of law,
and to be disarmed in his presence. The
ringleaders were placed under a strong
guard, and in the presence of the whole
army he addressed the offenders in an eloquent and feeling manner, impressing on
them their duties as citizens and soldiers,
and the *certainty of death* if they continued
to disobey their officers and remained in
that mutinous spirit, equally disgraceful to
them and hazardous to the sacred interests
they had marched to defend. Disorder was
instantly checked, and, after a short con-
finement, those under imprisonment were
released; the whole company was ever after
as exemplary in deportment and conduct as
any troop in the army.

On June 5, 1776, Mercer was promoted

and made a Brigadier-General in the Continental Army, of which the following correspondence gives evidence:

"President of Congress to General Mercer, Philadelphia, June 6, 1776. Sir: I am directed by Congress to inform you that they yesterday appointed you a Brigadier-General in the armies of the United Colonies, and that they request you will immediately on receipt hereof set out for headquarters at New York; for which purpose I am commanded to forward you this by express. Should you take Philadelphia in your way, I must beg you will do me the favor to call at my house, as it is highly probable I shall have something in charge from Congress ready for you at that time. I do myself the pleasure to enclose your commission; and have the honor to be, sir,
"Your most obedient and very humble servant,
"J. HANCOCK, President.
"To   Brigadier-General   Mercer,   Virginia."

"Williamsburg, June 15, 1776.
"Sir: I had the honor yesterday to receive your letter of the 6th inst., together with a commission, appointing me a Briga-

dier-General in the army of the United Colonies.

"Give me leave, sir, to request of you to present to the honorable Congress my most grateful acknowledgements in this distinguished mark of their respect.

"I was on duty with part of my regiment before Gwinn's Island, where Lord Dunmore has taken possession, when your instructions reached me; in consequence of this I shall use my utmost diligence, after settling the accounts of my regiment, to wait on you in Philadelphia. I have the honor to be, sir,

"Your most obedient, humble servant,

"HUGH MERCER.

"To the Honorable John Hancock, Esquire."

General Washington soon afterward appointed him to take full command of the troops at Paulus Hook, and charged him with the duty of directing the movement of a large detachment of Pennsylvania Militia and of protecting that point against a threatening invasion by the enemy from Staten Island. The latter part of the year 1776 the Colonists, with bated breath, feared the end of their struggle for liberty had come. New York and Rhode Island had been left in the hands of the British. Washington slowly withdrew from New Jersey, stubbornly disputing every effort to bring on an engagement; he crossed the Delaware; as the Royalists approached he retreated; at last he took refuge beyond that river, and for a distance of many miles he withdrew all the boats on its shores to its right bank, in order to impede Cornwallis in case he attempted to cross. The army of the Colonists was poorly clad, many of them barefooted; without tents, with few blankets, and very scantily fed, they were confronted by Cornwallis with a splendidly equipped army, well provisioned and clothed.

The British Hessians were then in possession of Trenton, and had to a large extent the practical control of the State of New Jersey. Sir William Howe boasted that Philadelphia would fall when the Delaware became frozen. At this critical juncture, on Christmas night, Washington crossed the Delaware amid a blinding storm of snow and sleet. His passage became much impeded by floating ice, but with the rallying cry of "Victory or death," he executed that brilliant movement on December 26, at Trenton, which caused the loyal though much depressed pa-

triots to renew their fast-wasting courage.

By this coup-de-main, Washington captured in the battle fought in Trenton about
one thousand stands of arms, one thousand
prisoners, and many stores of ammunition,
with a large amount of provisions and
clothing. This, with a bounty of ten dollars in gold to his troopers, restored fresh
confidence in his rank and file, and caused
the Continentals whose term of enlistment
was about to expire to remain under the
new flag of the Colonists for some weeks
longer. For this brilliant victory historians, with one accord, give credit and glory
to Mercer. Major Armstrong, his aide-de-
camp, who was present at a council of officers, and who was with Mercer at the cross-
ing of the Delaware, is authority for the
statement that Mercer suggested this expedition, fraught with so much peril and
uncertainty.

General Howe, who was amazed at
Washington's intrepid boldness, and
stunned by his great success, immediately
ordered Cornwallis by a forced march to
stop this onward advance. About five thousand men were pushed to Trenton, while a
larger body of men was held in reserve;
and on January 2d they met the advance

line of the Continental Army at Laurens-
ville. The British drove them back, and
about sunset of that day reached Trenton.
Washington, having carefully guarded the
ford and bridge, drew up his army beyond
the Assanpenk. This skirmish caused a
great loss in killed and wounded, and the
fate of the struggling Colonies was held
tremblingly in the balance. Had Cornwallis forced the fight that night with his vastly
superior and much better equipped troops,
it is possible that the fate of the Colonists
would have been sealed. He was urged to
make the attack, but refused, giving as an
excuse the fatigue of his troops, saying
"that he had the old fox just where he
wanted him, and would catch him in the
morning," a morning which never came to
him, so far as catching the "old fox" was
concerned.

Washington was now confronted with
great peril. The army of Cornwallis in
front and the Delaware in the rear, retreat
was impossible; an open engagement was
nearly certain to result in defeat; and defeat at this pivotal point in the life of the
Colonies meant the destruction of their
government and death to their hope for
that liberty for which they longed and had
suffered and sacrificed so much. At a coun-

cil of war held in General Mercer's headquarters that night, the determination and decision was reached to withdraw the Continental forces from in front of the enemy and go around him and attack the detachment then at Princeton; for by the Providence of God, the roads were made passable by being frozen, or else such a perilous expedition could not have been accomplished.

The pickets of the two armies were within two hundred yards of one another, and only a small stream, called the Assanpenk, was between them. In order to deceive the enemy, a long line of fire was kept up in Washington's front while his army was slowly on its way to Princeton, and thus deceived, the enemy slept. The "old fox" had escaped, as Cornwallis, much to his dismay, found in the morning.

A woman guided the Continental Army on that march beset with so many perils and difficulties. A woman! Her loyalty, her devotion, her sacrifice, and her sufferings for the cause of the Colony have given and shall ever give her all honor, praise, and gratitude.

Washington passed safely around the post of General Leslie at Maidenhead, but his progress was so slow that it was sunrise when he reached Stonybrook, about two miles from Princeton. He formed his column at the Quaker meeting house, which is still well preserved, at Princeton. The van and rearguard was composed of Continental soldiers who had bared their breasts to many a storm of shot and shell; the center was composed of troops who were first baptized with fire at Trenton. Washington ordered forward a detachment of about four hundred men under Mercer, consisting of the First Virginia Regiment, Shamwood's Regiment from Maryland, and Colonel Haslett's Delaware Regiments, with Neal's Battery, to seize a bridge at Worth's Mill. This detachment marched to the left from the road that leads along the brook, while Washington took a by-road to the right, in the rear of the Clark house; this road led directly to Princeton.

The Seventeenth, the Fortieth, and the Fifty-fifth British regiments, and three troops of Dragoons, had slept that night at Princeton, and had already begun their march to Trenton. The night had been dark and dreary, and the morning was severely cold; the Seventeenth Regiment having crossed the bridge, occupied a hill beyond it.

Mercer's presence was revealed at day-

The Quaker Meeting House, Princeton, New Jersey

break, and Mawhood at once counter-marched his regiment and crossed the bridge at Worth's Mill before Mercer could reach it, each side being surprised by the presence of the other. Each army tried to gain the high ground west of Clark's house. The Colonists reached it first, and from be-hind a worm fence opened fire, which was quickly responded to by the British.

The British troops charged after the third volley, and the Colonists were driven back in disorder before a bayonet charge from a force vastly superior in numbers. At this point General Mercer dismounted from his horse, which had been disabled, and tried vainly to rally his men; while he was doing so, he was knocked down by the butt-end of a musket in the hand of a Brit-ish trooper, who demanded that he should surrender, which he refused to do. He was then bayoneted and left for dead on the battle-field. (This spot has been marked by the erection of a white pillar.)

As soon as Washington heard this firing, he ordered forward the Pennsylvania Mi-litia and Moulder's Battery to the assist-ance of Mercer; thus reinforced, the flight of the Continentals was stopped, and the British were made to halt in their pursuit. At this critical moment Washington appeared in person, and taking in the situation of affairs at a glance, he waved his hat and cheered on his troops. Washington was now between the firing lines of both armies, and was in great danger and great peril. Moulder's Battery poured volley after volley into the ranks of the enemy, and the roar of musketry followed, as the brave Rhode Islanders and the Virginia Seventh swung, with other Continentals, into line, causing the enemy to break and fly, followed by victorious shouts from the American Army.

As the smoke of battle cleared away, it revealed Washington unharmed. Colonel Fitzgerald, his aide-de-camp, galloped to his side and said, ''Thank God, your excellency is safe!'' Washington replied, ''Away, my dear Colonel, and bring up the troops; the day is our own.''

The rout of the British was complete. Mawhood escaped with some of his scattered and shattered troops to Maidenhead. Some fled up Stonybrook; many were captured by a body of cavalry from Philadelphia.

General St. Clair met on this retreat the Fifty-fifth Regiment of British soldiers and quickly put them to flight; a portion of the Fortieth Regiment, which had not been in

The Battlefield of Princeton

the engagement, took refuge in Nassau Hall, Princeton, and were captured.

And thus on the morning of January 3, 1777, the Battle of Princeton, which was of short duration, but momentous of great results, was fought and won; and the shout of victory that commenced there was not hushed until at Yorktown the end came—an end which marks the beginning of our Republic, which is to-day the wonder of the world.

It is needless and unnecessary in this biography of General Mercer to recount the further movements, marches, and countermarches of Washington and his army. In this battle General Mercer, "who seems to have excited the brutality of the British by the gallantry of his resistance," was stabbed by their bayonets in seven different parts of his body, and they inflicted on his head many blows with the butt-end of their muskets, only ceasing this butchery when they believed him dead.

As soon after the battle as possible, General Mercer was removed to an adjacent farmhouse, owned by Mr. Clark, where Mrs. Clark and her daughter tenderly nursed him, being assisted by Major Lewis, who was delegated by General Washington to go there for that purpose. Dr. Rush, of

Philadelphia, and Dr. Archibald Alexander, of Augusta County, Virginia, who was then a surgeon of the Virginia troops, were at Mercer's bedside doing everything possible to alleviate his sufferings, which were intense and acute. Their services and ministrations were without avail, for on January 12, 1777, he died in the arms of Major Lewis. The angel of death wooed him to a brighter and better land, and the recording angel wrote in the great book, "Well done."

He had willingly sacrificed his life for the liberties of the people of his adopted land.

"For whether on the scaffold high,
  Or in the battle's van,
The noblest death that man can die
  Is when he dies for man."

The Clarke House, Princeton, where General Mercer died

CHAPTER V

DESIRING to give the full benefit of what others thought and said of General Mercer and the great value of his services to the struggling Colonies, it cannot be thought inappropriate for me to reproduce here what has already been written of him, especially by those who were near him in the times of which they wrote. Among those was General James Wilkinson, who says:

"The first fire was delivered by General Mercer, which the enemy returned with a volley and a sudden charge; many of our men being armed with rifles, were forced, after the third round, to abandon the fence, and fled in disorder. On hearing the fire, General Washington directed the Pennsylvania Militia to support General Mercer, and in person led them on, with two pieces of artillery under Capt. Wm. Moulder, of the city of Philadelphia, who formed a battery on the right of Thomas Clark's house; the enemy pursued the detachment of General Mercer as far as the brow of the declivity, etc. At the time General Mercer engaged the Seventeenth Regiment, under Colonel Hand, and endeavored by a right movement to turn the enemy's left flank, etc.''

In this affair our numerical loss was inconsiderable—it did not exceed 30, and only 14 were buried in the field; but it was of great magnitude in worth and talents. Colonels Haslett and Porter, Major Morris, and Capt. Wm. Shippen were respected in their corps; Captains Fleming and Neal presented fair promise of professional excellence; but in General Mercer was lost a chief who, for education, experience, talents, disposition, integrity and patriotism, was second to no man but the Commander-in-Chief, and was qualified to fill the highest trusts of the country. The manner in which he was wounded is an evidence of the excess to which the common soldiery are liable in the heat of action, especially when irritated by the loss of favorite officers. His way being obstructed, when advancing, by a post and rail fence in front of the orchard, it may be presumed that the General dismounted voluntarily, for he was on foot when the troops in the front hesitated, became confused, and soon gave way, while the few regulars in the rear could not check the dastardly retreat. Ere the for-

tune of the day was changed and victory
perched on the patriot standard, the heroic
Mercer fell. Rushing forward to rally his
broken troops, and stimulating them by
voice and example, his horse was shot from
under him, and he fell, dangerously wounded, among the columns of the advancing
enemy. Being thus dismounted, he was instantly surrounded by a number of British
soldiers, with whom, when they refused him
quarter, he fought desperately with drawn
sword until he was completely overpow-
ered. Excited to brutality by the gallantry
of his resistance, they stabbed him with
their bayonets in seven different parts of
his body, and inflicted many blows on his
head with the butt-ends of their muskets;
nor did they cease their butchery until they
believed him to be a crushed and mangled
corpse. Nine days after the battle, he died
in the arms of Major George Lewis, of the
army, the nephew of General Washington,
whom the uncle had commissioned to watch
over the last moments of his expiring
friend. His latter hours were soothed by
the skillful and affectionate attendance of
the distinguished Dr. Rush. He complained
much of his head, and frequently remarked
to his surgeon that *"there* was the principal danger,'' and Dr. Rush, in speaking of

his patient's suffering, always ascribed his death more to the blows on the head than to the bayonet wounds, although several of these were attended with extreme danger.

In a small house not far distant from the blood-red plain of carnage and death, but far away from the soothing consolations of domestic affection, this distinguished martyr of liberty breathed his last.

The mangled body was removed under a military escort from Princeton to Philadelphia, and exposed a day in the Coffee house, with the idea of exciting by that mournful spectacle the indignation of the people. The Pennsylvania *Evening Post* for January 18, 1777, has thus recorded his death and funeral obsequies: ''Last Sunday evening, died, near Princeton, of the wounds he received in the engagement at that place on the 3rd instant, Hugh Mercer, Esquire, Brigadier-General in the Continental Army. On Wednesday his body was brought to this city, and on Thursday buried on the south side of Christ Church, with military honors, attended by the Committee of Safety, the members of the Assembly, gentlemen of the army, and a number of the most respectable inhabitants of this city. The uniform character, exalted abilities, and intrepidity of this illustrious officer will render his name equally dear to America, with the liberty for which she is now contending, to the latest posterity.''

The battles of Trenton and Princeton, in which General Mercer fought and bled unto death, were the most brilliant and fortunate victories won in the War of the Revolution. The question of our independence was now no longer a matter of doubt. General Mercer's elevated character, lofty heroism, and brutal murder excited a deep and affectionate sympathy throughout all the Colonies. General Washington, in an official letter to the Continental Congress, thus alluded to Generals Mercer and Warren, Congress having, on April 7, 1777, resolved that a monument should be erected at Boston to the memory of General Warren, and one at Fredericksburg to General Mercer:

''The honors Congress has decreed to the memory of Generals Warren and Mercer afford me the highest pleasure. Their character and fortitude had a just claim to every mark of respect, and I heartily wish that every officer of the United States, emulating their virtues, may by their actions secure to themselves the same right to the grateful tributes of their country.''

On January 15, 1777, Washington wrote to Mr. Joseph Reed:

"When you see General Mercer, be so good as to present my best wishes to him—and congratulations (if the state of his health will admit of it) on his recovery from death. You may assure him that nothing but the confident assertion to me that he was either dead, or within a few minutes of dying, and that he was put into as good a place as I could remove him to, prevented his seeing me after the action and pursuit at Princeton."

When that letter was written the hero of Princeton had passed to the Great Beyond. A further evidence and expression of the high estimation in which General Mercer was held by Washington is found in a letter from the latter to General Livingston, dated from headquarters, July 6, 1776, 5 o'clock P. M., in which he wrote:

"General Mercer has just set off for Jersey. In his experience and judgment you may repose great confidence. He will proceed to Amboy after conferring with you. You will please to keep me constantly informed of the proceedings of the enemy, and be assured of every assistance and attention."

In the Journal of the Continental Congress for June 3 and July 19, 1776, what was known as the Flying Camp was constituted of ten thousand men, to be put under the command of such a Continental officer as General Washington should direct, and by his direction they assembled at Amboy, New Jersey, under the command of General Mercer.

General Washington, in another letter to General Livingston, of date July 5, 1776, referring to Mercer said: "His judgment and experience may be depended on;" and on January 5, 1777, in his official report to Congress, of the Battle of Princeton, after describing the battle and the capture of prisoners, etc., he said: "This piece of good fortune is counterbalanced by the loss of the brave and worthy General Mercer."

Nothing is needed further to show how the great Washington regarded Hugh Mercer, and to this I will add what was said of him by Lafayette on his last visit to this country.

The conversation in a brilliant company turning on the prominent men of the Revolution, one of the company observed to him that he, General Lafayette, was, of course, acquainted with General Mercer, not recollecting that Lafayette did not arrive in the United States until after the Battle of Princeton. "Oh, no," said the General, "you know that Mercer fell in January,

1777, and I reached the United States in the ensuing spring; but on my arrival I found the army and whole country so full of his name that an impression has been always left on my mind since that I was personally acquainted with him.''

At Princeton the high tide of the Revolution was reached. Before then, gloom had settled on the cause of the Colonies. The Tories, with their ''I told you so,'' predicted and prophesied a humiliating defeat, and the loyal Colonists began to doubt and despair. After that battle the bright sunshine of hope settled on this fair land of ours, and from that point the army of Washington fought to conquer; for the victory of Princeton not only encouraged the doubting and despairing rebels, as the Colonists were called, but it brought to them the recognition and alliance of France. That victory, however, was dearly gained, for amidst the exultant charge of our victorious legions could be heard the dying groans of that pure patriot—the brave and gallant Mercer.

''What death could finer laurel buy?
    What grander ending can there be
Than for a noble man to die
    To help to make his country free?

Although the day was dearly bought,
   'Twas there the Tyrant's doom was
      sealed,
And not in vain the fight was fought
   When Mercer fell on Princeton Field.

"His sword will waste away with rust,
   And tho' 'twere wrapped in cloth of
      gold,
Within the grave his precious dust
   In time will mingle with the mold;
But he, himself, is canonized,
   If saintly deeds such fame can give,
For long as Liberty is prized
   HUGH MERCER'S NAME SHALL SURELY
      LIVE."

January 28, 1841; Mrs George W. Morgan, of Philadelphia
sented to the St. Andrews Society of that city, the sword of
neral Hugh Mercer. The sword had been handed to Brig.
neral Jacob Morgan, Jr., who had, since he was 15 yrs
age, and knew Gen. Mercer at Fort Duquesne, where th
ught side by side, and in the Frontier Forts of Penna.,
ith his equally valorous father, Colonel Jacob Morgan
Morgantown, Berks Co., Penna.; known his fellow-
ficer who was at his side when he was lying at
this door and bid him carry on the good fight with hi
oop. "Mercer died in the arms" of the bosom of his frien
t only Major Lewis, — but of:
Brig. Gen. Jacob Morgan, Jr., 1741 – Sept 18, 1802. Buried
hrist Church Yd., Phila., Pa. Served (Rev War) Phila. B
ssociators, and First Bn. Phila. Militia, becoming
n Mustr. into State 1780.

CHAPTER VI

On January 31, 1777, the Continental
Congress passed the following resolution:
"That a committee of four be appointed to
consider what honors are due to the memory of General Mercer, who died on the
12th instant, of wounds received on the 3d
of the same month, in fighting against the
enemies of American liberty, near Princeton." The members of that committee were
the Hon. Messrs. Rush, Heynard, Page, and
S. Adams. On April 8, 1777, that committee reported "That a monument be
erected to the memory of General Mercer
at Fredericksburg, in the State of Virginia,
with the following inscription:

Sacred to the memory of
HUGH MERCER,
Brigadier-General in the Army of
The United States.
He died on the 12th of January, 1777,
of the wounds he received on the
3rd of the same month,
Near Princeton, in New Jersey,
Bravely defending the
Liberties of America.
The Congress of the United States,
In testimony of his virtues and their
gratitude,
Have caused this monument to be erected."

The report of the committee was, however, never executed. Under that resolution no monument was ever built; why, no
one knows. Nations, like some individuals,
soon forget. For more than a century did
this Republic fail in its duty to the memory
of the gallant Mercer. At last the conscience, as well as the sense of justice, of
the nation was aroused. Hence by an act
of Congress, approved June 28, 1902, the
resolution of 1777 was directed by Congress
to be carried into effect, and at Fredericksburg, in the State of Virginia, there has
been a monument erected to perpetuate the
fame and name of Hugh Mercer. And it

is well, "lest we forget, lest we forget."
The same epitaph is engraved on this monument that was prescribed in the resolutions of 1777. The City of Philadelphia
paid the memory of Mercer a great tribute
by giving his remains a public funeral,
which it is said 30,000 people attended. He
was buried in the graveyard of Christ
Church. In 1817 his son visited his grave;
the old sexton—a Mr. Dolley—who had attended the funeral of the General, was
there alone. Under the grass on the south
side of the brick enclosure was found a
plain and unadorned marble slab, inscribed
"Gl. M. In memory of Gen'l Hugh Mercer,
who fell at Princeton, January 3rd, 1777."
The St. Andrew's Society afterward removed his remains to the Laurel Hill Cemetery and erected a monument to his memory, which was dedicated with imposing
ceremonies on Thursday, November 26,
1840; on which occasion Wm. B. Reed,
Esq., grandson of Adjutant-General Reed,
of the Revolution, delivered a beautiful address. General Mercer had joined the St.
Andrew's Society in Philadelphia, in 1757.
On the front die of this monument, etc., is
the following inscription:

The Monument to Gen. Hugh Mercer at Fredericksburg, Va.

OPPOSITE P. 66

Dedicated to the memory of
GENERAL HUGH MERCER,
Who fell
For the sacred cause
of
Human Liberty
and
American Independence,
in
The Battle of Princeton.
He poured out his blood for a generous
principle.

Left-hand side of die:

The St. Andrew's Society
of Philadelphia
Offer this humble tribute
To the memory of
An illustrious brother.
When a grateful posterity shall bid the
trophied Memorial rise to the martyrs who
sealed with their blood the Charter of an
Empire's Liberties, there shall not be want-
ing a monument to him whom
Washington
Mourned as "The Worthy and Brave
MERCER."

Right-hand side of die:

General Mercer, a physician of Fredericksburg, in Virginia, was distinguished for his skill and learning, his gentleness and decision, his refinement and humanity, his elevated honour and his devotion to the great cause of civil and religious liberty.

In the historical paintings of the Battle of Princeton by Peale, at Princeton, and by Trumbull at New York, General Mercer is given a prominent position. And the states of Pennsylvania, Kentucky, Virginia, and New Jersey, have by solemn and appropriate acts of their respective Legislatures, named a county "Mercer" in his honor. On October 1, 1897, a bronze tablet was unveiled in Princeton, bearing this inscription:

"To the memory of General Hugh Mercer, the revered martyr of American Independence. Born in Scotland in 1720; educated as a physician; emigrated to America in 1747; was appointed by Congress, June 5th, 1776, a Brigadier-General in the American Army; was mortally wounded at the Battle of Princeton, January 3rd, 1777; and died in the house now standing near this spot January 12th, 1777. This tablet was

The Grave of General Mercer in Laurel Hill Cemetery,
Philadelphia, Pa., with Monument Erected
by St. Andrew's Society

OPPOSITE P. 70

erected by the Mercer Engine Company No. 3 of Princeton, N. J., October 1st, 1897, at the semi-centennial celebration.''

On this occasion Judge Beverly R. Wellford, of Richmond, Va., and Dr. Henry C. Cameron, of Princeton, made eloquent and appropriate historical orations.

In November, 1899, the Hon. Henry W. Green, of Trenton, N. J., presented a handsome portrait of General Mercer to the Mercersburg Academy of Pennsylvania; and in doing so, among other things, said:

''His life record shows him as a soldier, brave and courageous; as a physician, learned in his profession; as a scholar, well read and of generous attainments; as a patriot, pure and impulsive; as a Christian, self-sacrificing and true. Few lives illume the page of national history with kindlier glow than that of Mercer. Fortunate the town with such a namesake; honored the school that bears his name; glorified the nation in whose cause he laid down that most precious of his possessions—his life.''

Hugh Mercer was an alumnus of Marschal College and the University of Aberdeen, Scotland, and this university recognizes him as one of its most illustrious students. In its annual list of honored alumni, he is one of the three chosen to represent

the profession of arms; the other two being
Field-Marshal James Keith, the distinguished officer in the service of Frederick
the Great, and Sir James Outram, the
"Bayard of India."

Congress, on motion of Thomas Jefferson, in 1784 made an appropriation for the
education of General Mercer's youngest
son, Hugh, who died at his residence, "The
Sentry Box," December 2, 1853. Another
son, John, a distinguished lawyer, died
September 30, 1817; and his only daughter, Anna Gordon, who married Robert Patton, died in Fredericksburg, Va., May 12,
1832. General Hugh W. Mercer, of Savannah, Ga., a gallant officer in the Confederate Army, was a grandson of General Mercer, and the late John M. Patton, another
grandson, was a member of Congress from
the Fredericksburg District under Jackson's administration, and was acting-Gov-
ernor of Virginia in 1840.

Now as the end of the story of the life
of Hugh Mercer in this work approaches,
by way of recapitulation it behooves us to
ask, What were the most attractive and potential elements of that life? We would
say, Fidelity to principle, fixedness of purpose, faithfulness in the discharge of the
obligations imposed by citizenship, with a

fearlessness that knew no limitation when
duty and obligation joined in demanding
energetic action. To realize that this is
true, the reader need only be reminded of
what was accomplished by Mercer, and how
that accomplishment was brought about.
We find him at Culloden obeying every in-
spiration of loyalty to Scotland and Scottish traditions when he championed the
cause of the Pretender. To have done oth-
erwise would have been contrary to every
dictate of duty as it was impressed on Scotland itself. When he became a resident of
America, on the frontier of Pennsylvania,
he felt himself obliged by the very highest
and holiest obligations of citizenship to im-
peril his life in many Indian wars in order
to preserve the lives and protect the homes
of the people among whom he lived. When
the tocsin of war sounded, and the Colonies "struck for liberty" and for freedom
from the intolerable and tyrannical aggressions of Great Britain, being impressed
with the right and righteousness of the
cause of the Colonies, he at once offered his
services in their behalf, gave up his life for
the cause which he espoused, and died that
liberty might live.

His life was a strenuous one, full of ex-
acting and unselfish work for others: As a

country doctor, ministering to the sick and comforting the suffering; as a Mason, teaching by precept and by example the cardinal doctrines of the craft, the fatherhood of God and the brotherhood of man; as a member of the church, expressing by his walk and conversation the faith he felt in the Savior of men, whom he humbly followed; as the head of his home, in the God-given capacity of husband and father, ever directing its affairs and executing its duties, making his home life spotless and stainless; as a citizen, evading no obligation and avoiding no demand imposed upon that citizenship. He was a soldier always, vigilant, obedient and loyal; an officer whose tactics were of the onward, never backward order, counselling against evacuation of strategic positions, even though it seemed impossible to retain them, with judgment that could be always relied on, said the great Washington. When confronted by seemingly insurmountable obstacles, he suggested movements by which superiority in numbers could be overridden by superiority in forethought and decisive action. He was brave without being desperate; he was a good disciplinarian without being a martinet. In his vocabulary there was no such word as "surrender." He was willing "to do, dare or die'' for the flag under which he enlisted; he unsheathed his sword in honor, and never was it dishonored to his dying day; he was the hero of Princeton, with no one to pluck that laurel from his brow, and is entitled to the glory that came from that victory which resulted in a Confederation of States that has made the Western Hemisphere the admiration and the wonder of the world. He is entitled to the gratitude of all liberty-loving America. His life was beautiful and complete in its symmetry, and was both a benediction and benefaction. The memory of such a man cannot perish from the face of the earth, but shall be as eternal as Truth.

CHAPTER VII

This narrative would not be complete
without a short story of the friends of
Hugh Mercer at Fredericksburg—his daily
associates, who communed with him at the
sessions of the Masonic Lodge; who sat
around the old open fireplace at the Rising
Sun tavern and talked with him about the
gossip of the town; who watched and waited
with him, in front of the post-office, for the
coming of the rumbling, rattling old stage
with its weekly mail and its belated news
from Williamsburg. It is not, however, my
purpose to write a biography of these people, but only a short sketch of them as their
lives touched that of Mercer's, and as these
distinguished people were connected and
associated with Fredericksburg; and, as
Washington stands in the forefront of this
nation's life, so he stands, peerless and
high above all others, in the life of this
town.

The Rising Sun Tavern, Fredericksburg, Virginia

GEORGE WASHINGTON

He who was "first in war, first in peace, and first in the hearts of his countrymen" was a very small boy when his father, Augustine Washington, died on his place, since called "The Washington Farm," opposite Fredericksburg. He went to school in that town, and in after-life referred to it as the town of his youth and maturing manhood. Just before the commencement of the Revolution, his mother and her family moved into the town. Washington, in his maturer years, visited his mother there frequently. He and his bride, en route from Williamsburg to Mount Vernon, came by Fredericksburg to receive, no doubt, his mother's blessing and benediction. He was the owner of several lots in the town. After the surrender of Cornwallis at Yorktown, Washington, impelled by the love and adoration which he had for her, determined that his first visit should be to his mother at Fredericksburg, and he came to her without delay. On that visit he was received with expressions of joy and gratitude by the people of the place, and was presented with an address of welcome and congratulations by the Town Council. On that occasion a grand ball was given in his honor, which he attended, accompanied by Lafayette and other distinguished officers. In those days the ball commenced at early candle-light. His aged mother, whom he escorted, left at nine o'clock. After seeing her safely home, he returned and danced the stately minuet with one of the Gregory girls, who was his cousin.

Washington was a member of Lodge No. 4, A. F. and A. M., the records of which lodge show that he was made a Mason November, 1752. On that date there was received from George Washington, for his entrance fee, two pounds and five shillings.

When in Fredericksburg he attended the services of St. George's Episcopal Church. It is related that on one of his visits after he had become great and famous, while attending the services of this church, it became overcrowded, that the old frame building gave evidences of being unsafe, and that a panic was only averted by the coolness of Washington himself.

His only sister, Bettie, who married Fielding Lewis, lived at a place called "Kenmore," then on the outskirts of the town.

Parson Weems locates Fredericksburg as the place where the great Washington

Kenmore, at Fredericksburg, where Major Lewis Lived

. threw a silver dollar across the Rappahannock River, and the farm just across the river and immediately opposite Fredericksburg as the place where the cherry tree and hatchet incident occurred. Although tradition says Washington read this life of himself by Weems, history does not record what he said about it. Perhaps he thought if he (Washington) could not tell a lie, the parson could, and did.

Mercer and Washington were close and intimate friends from the time they first met on the frontier of Pennsylvania until the death of Mercer at Princeton. They often met in old Fredericksburg, at the home of Washington's mother, in the lodge room, and at the old Rising Sun tavern. He who enters the town is constrained to stand reverently, with uncovered head, on ground around which cling holy memories of its most illustrious citizen.

JOHN PAUL JONES

John Paul was born July 6, 1747, in the parish of Kirkbean, Scotland. His brother, William Paul, had resided in Fredericksburg some time prior to 1760, and kept a grocery store in a house now standing at the corner of Prussia and Main streets.

The will of William Paul is recorded in Spottsylvania County, dated March 22, 1772, and probated November 16, 1774. In his will he wrote: "It is my will and desire that my lots and houses in this town be sold and converted into money, which I give and bequeath to my beloved sister, Mary Young, and her two oldest children, in the Parish of Kirkbean, in the stewarty of Galloway, North Britain, Scotland." And as this Mary Young was also sister of John Paul, it cannot possibly be doubted that William and John Paul were brothers. William Paul died in 1773, and is buried in old St. George's churchyard. Over his remains there is still standing a moss-covered stone, with the simple inscription: "William Paul, 1773."

Seven cities claimed Homer, dead, and three contended for Virgil; a greater number of American cities claim that John Paul had his home within their gates, but the record is against them. Fredericksburg, Virginia, was the one and only home of the great admiral in this country. One of his many biographers, as far back as 1823, locates him at Fredericksburg, at the home of his brother William.

During the Revolution he wrote to Baron Von Copelan: "America has been the country of my fond election since I was thirteen, when I first saw it." His first visit, therefore, to Fredericksburg was about 1760, and after remaining there for nearly four years he went back to Scotland. In "The National Portrait Gallery," published in 1833, it is stated, "In 1773 we find him (John Paul) in Fredericksburg, arranging the estate of his brother William, who had settled in Fredericksburg." In addition, the traditions and history of the town establish the unimpeachable fact that the illustrious hero of the sea had only one home in America—Fredericksburg. It was while living there that he added Jones to his name. The reason that moved him to do this is not known. Speculation and guesses abound, and authorities differ. There must have been some strong impelling cause, but it is locked in the mystery of a long silence.

While a resident of that town he received his commission as lieutenant in the Continental Navy. The splendid achievements of John Paul Jones are already so well known to the world that I will not attempt in so brief an article as this to narrate them or to give the story of his brilliant career.

His hand was the first to unfurl the Stars and Stripes on the high seas. As the commander of the Bon Homme Richard, his story is the pride of every boy in America. He was the only man who ever gave battle to the English on English soil. These things are within the knowledge of all. It is of his life in Fredericksburg that I write, and strive to redeem from the past those years of which so little has been written.

Mercer and Jones, both Scotchmen, were residents there at the same time, and it can scarcely be drawing on the imagination to picture these men of the Clans of old Scothand often meeting in social intercourse to talk of the land of their birth, being drawn together as friends and associates by the strong bond of their mother-country.

It was from Fredericksburg that Mercer went forth to make his name immortal, fighting the battles of the Colonies on land; and it was from there that John Paul Jones went to become illustrious by his great victories on the sea. The memories of both these great and illustrious men are cherished by old Fredericksburg, and will ever be cherished by her as long as the story of their lives shall live and Fredericksburg shall last.

John Paul Jones

OPPOSITE P. 82

GENERAL GEORGE WEEDON

George Weedon was the "mine host" of the Rising Sun tavern at Fredericksburg, whom our English traveler, heretofore mentioned, said was over-zealous in stirring up sedition in the Colonies. He was also postmaster there. The post-office was kept in the tavern. Weedon was appointed lieutenant-colonel of the regiment of which Mercer was the colonel, was promoted to its colonelcy on August 17, 1776, and was made a brigadier-general on February 24, 1777.

In the Battle of Brandywine, Weedon rendered conspicuous and valuable service while commanding a brigade in Greene's division, which checked the pursuit of the British and saved our army from utter and complete rout. He was a brave and brilliant commanding officer at the Battle of Germantown. In consequence of some dissatisfaction about rank, he left the army at Valley Forge, re-entering it in 1780; and in 1781 he was given the command of the Virginia Militia at Gloucester, which position he held at the surrender of Cornwallis at Yorktown.

General Weedon was the first president of the Virginia Branch of the Society of

Cincinnati, and was a member of Lodge
No. 4, A. F. and A. M., of which lodge Mercer was at one time the Master. After the
death of his brother-in-law, General Hugh
Mercer, General Weedon occupied "The
Sentry Box" on lower Main street; and
was appointed by the Court the guardian of
Mercer's children. He died in Fredericksburg in the early part of the last century.

The General wrote a song, entitled
"Christmas Day in '76," which was sung
at his festive board at each recurring
Christmas. A very interesting account of
this was given in a letter dated February
8, 1837, from Hugh Mercer, Esq., the son
of the General, to the grandfather of Judge
Beverly Wellford, of Richmond, and no
apology is offered for reproducing this
song in this memoir.

CHRISTMAS DAY IN '76

On Christmas Day in seventy-six
Our ragged troops, with bayonets fixed,
    For Trenton marched away.
The Delaware ice, the boats below,
The light obscured by hail and snow,
    But no signs of dismay.

Our object was the Hessian band
That dare invade fair Freedom's land,
    At quarter in that place.
Great Washington, he led us on,
With ensigns streaming with renown,
    Which ne'er had known disgrace.

In silent march we spent the night,
Each soldier panting for the fight,
    Though quite benumbed with frost.
Greene on the left at six began,
The right was with brave Sullivan,
    Who in battle no time lost.

Their pickets stormed; the alarm was
        spread;
The rebels, risen from the dead,
    Were marching into town.
Some scampered here, some scampered
        there,
And some for action did prepare;
    But soon their arms laid down.

Twelve hundred servile miscreants,
With all their colors, guns, and tents,
    Were trophies of the day.
The frolic o'er, the bright canteen
In center, front, and rear, was seen,
    Driving fatigue away.

And, brothers of the cause, let's sing
Our safe deliverance from a king
    Who strove to extend his sway.
And life, you know, is but a span;
Let's touch the tankard while we can,
    In memory of the day.

"Written by General George Weedon, of
the Revolutionary Army, who was in the
action at Trenton, and had charge of the
Hessian prisoners after the victory, which
prevented his being at Princeton a few
days after and taking part in that glorious
victory.

"My uncle and second father, General
Weedon, went through the whole Revolutionary War, commanding the American
troops on the Gloucester side of York River
during the siege of York and the surrender
of the British Army at that memorable
place. The brilliant victories at Trenton
and Princeton were won at the most gloomy
period of the great struggle for our independence; it was the crisis of the war, and
turned the scale in favor of our bleeding
country.   H. MERCER."

"My dear Sir: I have had much pleasure in writing out for you, as you request-
ed, the patriotic song of 'Christmas Day in
'76.' For many years after the Revolution

my uncle celebrated at 'The Sentry Box' (his residence, and now mine) the capture of the Hessians, by a great festival—a jubilee dinner, if I may so express myself—at which the Revolutionary officers then living here and in our vicinity, besides others of our friends, were always present. It was an annual feast, a day or so after Christmas Day, and the same guests always attended.

"Your father was, of course, a standing guest. I was young, and a little fellow, and was always drawn up at the table to sing 'Christmas Day in '76.'

"Two young servant boys he was bringing up as waiters in the family were posted at the door as sentinels, in military costumes, with wooden muskets on their shoulders; one he called Corporal Killbuck and the other Corporal Killdee. It was always a joyous holiday at 'The Sentry Box.'

"I am, my dear sir,
                "Most truly yours,
                                "H. MERCER."

JAMES MONROE

James Monroe was born in Westmoreland County, Virginia, April 28, 1758. He was educated at William and Mary College, graduating in 1776. On leaving that college he took up law for a profession; but being inspired by the martial fire that was then filling the breasts of the young men of that time, at the commencement of hostilities he offered his services and sword in the cause of the Colonies. He was made a lieutenant in the regiment which was commanded by Hugh Mercer, and was with Washington and Mercer when they crossed the Delaware. On December 26, 1776, he was wounded in the shoulder at Trenton, while leading the van of the army. On recovering from his wound he was appointed as an aide-de-camp on the staff of Lord Sterling, and was in the battles of Brandywine, Germantown and Monmouth.

After the war he again took up his residence in Fredericksburg. Under the laws then in force, in order to vote and hold office it was necessary to own property; and to meet that qualification, an uncle of Monroe, who was also a resident of Fredericksburg, made him a gift of a town lot, and thus he was enabled to exercise the great and inalienable right of an American citizen.

Monroe was at that time a member of the Fredericksburg Town Council, and a vestryman of St. George's Episcopal

"The Sentry Box," the Home of Mercer, Fredericksburg, Virginia

Church. When only twenty-four years of
age he was sent to Congress for the district
of which Fredericksburg constituted a part.
So it was brought about that Monroe, in the
Town Council of Fredericksburg, commenced a career which culminated in his
election to the Presidency.

Monroe was a continuous office-holder,
having been a town councilman, a member
of the Virginia Legislature, Governor of
that State, member of Congress, minister
to two foreign courts, senator, cabinet officer and President. And, what is to his
everlasting honor and credit, he executed
the trusts of these various and varied sta-
tions with faithfulness and efficiency. He
did his duty, and did it well, and has en-
shrined his name in America's history as
a patriotic citizen, and as a conscientious,
conservative and able officer.

The result of his life in dollars and cents
was that his poverty was to him a badge
of honor.

Monroe was much younger than Mercer,
but he doubtless was found on the outskirts
of the assembled and much excited patriots
around the old open fireplace at the Rising
Sun tavern, which tradition locates as a
meeting place of these worthies "in ye old-
en time" for the discussion of the removal

of the powder at Williamsburg by Dunmore, and other acts of England's intolerable tyranny, as well as to formulate methods and means to stop and stay the onward march of Great Britain's aggressions against the rights and liberties of the Colonies. And when the cry "To arms!" rang out over the land, young Monroe showed his faith by his works when he enlisted in the regiment of which his friend, Mercer, was colonel.

He was, however, destined to play a greater and more prominent part in the drama of life than Mercer. From a lieutenant he became the Commander-in-Chief of the army; from a member of the council of the town of Fredericksburg he became the Chief Executive of the Republic. Who knows how potential was the influence of Mercer on the life of Monroe, and how much, and how far, that influence shaped and molded his character, and thus brought about the illustrious career of Monroe? We only know that they were true and loyal friends.

MARY, THE MOTHER OF WASHINGTON

After the death of her husband, Augustine Washington, "Madam Washington," as she was called by her neighbors and friends, moved to Fredericksburg, and lived and died in the house now standing on the corner of Charles and Lewis streets.

The world pays its tribute to the memory of the mother of the "Father of His Country." President Andrew Jackson said that "the character of Washington was aided and strengthened, if not formed, by the care and precepts of his mother, who was remarkable for the vigor of her intellect and the firmness of her resolution."

Mrs. Washington was left in early life a widow, with the burden of a young and large family, and to the task of guarding and governing them she unselfishly devoted herself. She was a woman of much business ability, for her farm she managed with great skill and with profitable results. Tradition says she was rather inaccessible and somewhat exclusive, for she was in no sense a society woman. Mrs. Washington was intensely religious, a consistent member of St. George's Episcopal Church, and very charitable to the poor. Her hospitable home

was always open to her friends, among
whom was Hugh Mercer, who was a fre-
quent visitor there.

When Washington found himself the lau-
rel-crowned hero of the new Republic, he
came first to pay his homage and filial devotion to his revered mother. On that visit
he was accompanied by Lafayette and a
number of other distinguished military
men. She received him as a devoted mother should receive a dutiful son. In that
reception Washington the hero, to her, had
no part. She was proud of her great son,
proud because of his greatness, but prouder
still, no doubt, as she remembered her part
in making that son great.

He escorted her to the Peace Ball before
mentioned. At nine o'clock she said it was
time for old people to go home, and she
went.

Washington sent a special messenger to
his mother, it is said, to give her the glad
tidings of the surrender of Cornwallis. An
old gentleman once told the writer of this
brief memoir that when that messenger
dashed up the deserted streets of Fredericksburg a Mr. Keiger, then a very young
but precocious boy, was urged by some
older ones standing on the street corner to
go up to Madam Washington and get the

The Home of Mary, the Mother of Washington, Fredericksburg, Virginia

OPPOSITE P. 92

news. Keiger went; Mrs. Washington was
in her garden; he watched and waited until
she had opened the letter with a pair of
scissors attached to her waist by a cord,
then turning, she said, "My young man,
what is it you want?" He told her. She
said. "Tell the gossips that George has
sent me word that Lord Cornwallis has sur-
rendered at Yorktown."

Lafayette, on his visit, called on the
mother of his illustrious chief; he wrote
home to France quite a lengthy account of
that visit. Mrs. Washington met him at
the door of her residence; he introduced
himself. "Walk right in," said the Madam.
"I am glad to see you, for George has told
me all about you." He was ushered into
the parlor, and refreshed the inner man
with her home-made ginger cake and her
home-brewed rum punch; and he went from
that simple country home declaring that he
was glad to say he had seen in her a splendid old Virginia matron.

In appearance, Mrs. Washington was of
medium height, and rather stout in her old
age, but carried herself with great dignity.
For a number of years she suffered from
a very painful disease. On August 25, 1789,
she died. In her last illness she was attended by Doctors Mortimer and Hall. The

funeral ceremonies were held in St. George's Episcopal Church, August 28, 1789. On the day of the funeral all business was suspended in the town; the church bells tolled. The whole population wended its way solemnly and reverently to pay its last sad tribute to the memory of a friend and neighbor. She was buried on the Kenmore farm, then owned and occupied by her daughter, Mrs. Fielding Lewis, in a spot she herself had selected for that purpose, near what are now known as the Oratory Rocks, where she frequently sat with her grandchildren and read her Bible.

When the sad tidings of her death was conveyed to Congress, resolutions of sympathy for President Washington, and a tribute to her memory, were passed. This deeply touched Washington, who responded in a note of thanks, adding: ''I attribute all of my success in life to the moral, intellectual and physical education which I received from my mother.'' No grander tribute was ever paid by a great man to his mother than that, and the world, well knowing how much was accomplished by him, can readily pay its homage to the memory of this great and good woman, for—

"Methinks we see thee as in olden time,
Simple in garb, majestic and serene,
Unmoved by pomp and circumstance,
Inflexible, and with a Spartan zeal
Repressing vice, and making folly
      grave."

In 1833 the erection of a monument over
the grave of this most illustrious of American women was commenced, but never com-
pleted. Congress was importuned, but
failed to act, although it had promised in
1789, by solemn resolution, to build a monument to mark the spot where sleeps the
mother of Washington.

On October 21, 1889, the following appeal
was made by the wife of this writer:

"AN APPEAL IN BEHALF OF THE MARY
      WASHINGTON MONUMENT

"Amid great pomp and ceremony the
corner-stone of the monument to the memory of Mary Washington, the mother of
'The Father of this Republic,' was laid in
1833. The erection of the monument over
the grave of this most illustrious of American women was voluntarily undertaken by
a philanthropic and patriotic citizen, Silas

Burrows, of New York. Mr. Burrows died before its completion. It is now in an unfinished and dilapidated condition.

"Congress has been again and again appealed to and importuned. Favorable legislation has been promised, but this incomplete monument crumbles and decays. Shall the memory of the mother of the great Washington longer be neglected? In every State of this Union monuments mark with emphasis the veneration with which George Washington is held by a grateful republic, and at the Capitol of the nation there is one that towers above all the rest; but nowhere is there recognition made of the mother. Her very grave at this place is marked only by an unsightly pile of marble. Shall this neglect continue?

"Mrs. Washington was an uncommon woman. It is recorded of her that 'she was of strong will, splendid judgment, untiring energy, and without pretension,' and from these elements she molded her great son, taught him to become great, equipped him with attributes essential to greatness.

"She lived, during the Revolutionary War, in Fredericksburg; died, and was buried here at the spot she herself had selected for that purpose. Shall the grave of Mary

Washington be allowed to remain longer in a condition which is the reminder of the forgetfulness, rather than the gratitude, of our people? Remember that the grave of Washington himself is held as a very Mecca to which all liberty-loving people can make their pilgrimage—the work of the faithful and devoted women of this land. And it is proposed that an organization shall at once be formed, having for its object the erection of a monument over the grave of George Washington's mother at this place.

"Will the women of this Republic respond to this appeal? Are they not willing to undertake this patriotic work?

"To the end that steps may be immediately taken, it is intended to obtain a charter of incorporation of the Mary Washington Memorial Association, to have a president, one vice-president in each State, and other usual and necessary officers, all women. It is also suggested that the ladies of America, on February 22, 1890, shall in every State make some organized effort to raise the necessary funds. The writer of this requests that the papers give circulation to this appeal, and she will be glad to hear from any ladies who desire to take an active interest in this patriotic purpose.

"MRS. JOHN T. GOOLRICK.
"Fredericksburg, Va., Oct. 15, 1889."

In response, largely to that appeal, or in part at least as a result of it, the National Mary Washington Monument Association was organized, composed of patriotic women of America, and a stately, imposing monument stands sentinel over the grave of Mrs. Washington. On one side of it is inscribed, "Erected by Her Country-women." Just here it will not be irrelevant to record an incident. A verdant woman visited this monument and read "Erected by Her Countrywomen." "Thank the Lawd!" she said, "that no city wimen had nothing to do with this monument." On the other side of this splendid granite shaft is inscribed in raised letters this epitaph:

"Mary, the Mother of Washington."

LODGE NO. 4, A. F. AND A. M.

Past Master Bro. S. J. Quinn, of Fredericksburg, has compiled a very interesting history of this Lodge. From it we find that it was organized September 1, 1752. It

The Monument to Mary, the Mother of Washington, Fredericksburg, Virginia

has had among its membership many good men and true, many who became illustrious besides George Washington, Hugh Mercer and George Weedon, of whose membership in that Lodge we have heretofore made mention. Its records are quaint and curious, and as an illustration of this, we extract from its proceedings as follows:

"On December 19, 1755, it was resolved by unanimous consent of the Lodge, that the treasurer shall, at his discretion, purchase on account of this Lodge six lottery tickets, and the numbers of them to be returned to the Lodge and made a minute of." And tradition says that these tickets were signed by the illustrious brother, George Washington, who was president of the company.

On April 15, 1769, "on motion of Brother Alexander Woodron, it was resolved, that the stewarts of this Lodge, for the time being, shall for the future provide liquors, candies, and all other necessaries for the use of the Lodge." About this time two demijohns, one called "Jachen," full of Jamaica rum, and the other called "Boaz," full of Holland gin, with an old-fashioned loaf of sugar, were kept in the ante-room for the refreshment of the brethren; and tradition hath it, that some of the brothers were content to tarry in the ante-room and never got any farther.

"On December 27, 1756, being the anniversary of our Patron Saint John, the Lodge assembled, attended by several visiting brothers, and went in procession to the church, where we heard a most excellent sermon preached by our worthy Brother James Marye, after which we returned in procession to the Lodge, where our worthy Master returned the thanks of the Lodge to our worthy Brother James Marye for so good a sermon.

"The Lodge being closed, the evening was spent very agreeably with a Ball."

On the second Sunday in December, 1799, after the death of General Washington, Lodge No. 4 met in a Lodge of sorrow. The Grand Master of Virginia, who was a member of that Lodge and citizen of Fredericksburg, Benjamin Day, made an address, from which we quote in part:

"We are now, brethren, assembled to pay the last sad tribute of affection and respect to the eminent virtues and exemplary conduct that adorned the character of our worthy deceased brother, George Washington. He was early initiated in this venerable Lodge, in the mysteries of our ancient and honorable profession, and having

General George Washington as a Mason and Member of
Lodge No. 4, A. F. and A. M., Fredericksburg, Virginia

held it in the highest and most just veneration, the fraternal attention we now show
to his memory is the more incumbent
upon us.''

After these memorial exercises in the
Lodge room, the Lodge went in procession
to St. George's Episcopal Church, where
religious services were held.

On Sunday, November 28, 1824, General
Lafayette, with his son, George Washington Lafayette, and Colonel La Vassem, visited that Lodge. Lafayette on this occasion
was made an Honorary Member, and in response to an address of welcome the Mar-
quis said:

''The pleasure I ever feel in our fraternal meetings cannot but be enhanced by the
consideration, that in this city the first lessons of childhood, and in this Lodge the
first lessons of Masonry, were conferred
upon the man who was first in all our
hearts.'' * * *

This old Lodge has many valuable relics
and mementos of the old times; among
them, a portrait of Washington painted
from life by Sully, and the Holy Bible upon
which Washington, Mercer and Weedon
were obligated as Masons.

This historic Lodge, the Alma Mater in
Masonry of distinguished and illustrious

men, feels proud of its record, as well as
of its roll of honor; for it has always been
faithful and true to the sacred principles
and tenets of the order, ever practicing
and proclaiming as its holy mission the ele-
vation and ennoblement of mankind.

APPENDIX

GENEALOGICAL NOTES ON THE DESCENDANTS

OF

REV. JOHN MERCER OF KINNELLAN
1650-1676.

John Mercer 1 was minister of Kinnellan in Aberdeenshire, Scotland, from 1650 to 1676, when he resigned (in June) because of infirmity. He died August 7, 1677. John Mercer of Kinnellan married Lilias Row. She was the great-granddaughter of John Row, the Reformer. (See *The Scottish Nation* by William Anderson, Vol. III, p. 380.)

The children of John Mercer (1) and Lilias Row, his wife, were:

1. John Mercer 2. Baptized January 8, 1654, at Old Machar. Died young.

2. Agnes 2 (or Annas). Baptized January 20, 1656. Polled, 1696, at Todlay, Parish of Alva.

3. Thomas Mercer 2. Baptized January 20, 1658. Polled, 1696. He was married twice. His first wife was Anna Raite. The marriage contract is dated July 13, 1681. His second wife was Isabel.

The children of THOMAS MERCER 2 (5) were:

1. Lilias Mercer 3. Polled 1696.
2. John Mercer 3. Polled 1696. Married Isabel Martin.
3. Margaret Mercer 3. Polled 1696.
4. Janet Mercer 3. Polled 1696. Married June 1, 1704, at Fyvie, to Robert Rait of Micklefalla.
5. Thomas Mercer 3. Baptized April 25, 1693. Polled 1696.
6. Christian Mercer 3. Baptized June 4, 1695. Polled 1696.
7. William Mercer 3. Baptized March 25, 1696. Married Anne, daughter of Sir Robert Munro of Foulis.

The children of John Mercer 3 (9) and Isabel Martin, his wife, were:

1. Elizabeth Mercer 4. Baptized December 10, 1710. Married Rev. James Wilson, minister of Glowerie, May 27, 1735.

2. John Mercer 4. Baptized March 27, 1717.

3. Thomas Mercer 4. Baptized October 17, 1721.

4. Isabel Mercer 4. Baptized June 15, 1723.

5. Agnes Mercer 4. Baptized May 20, 1725.

————

The children of WILLIAM MERCER 3 (14) and ANNE MUNRO 3 (15), his wife, were:

1. Margaret Mercer 4. Baptized June 8, 1724.

2. Hugh Mercer 4. Baptized January, 1726. Emigrated to America and married Isabella Gordon of Virginia. Wounded at Princeton, January 3, 1777, where he died on January 12th of the same year.

3. Isabel Mercer 4. Baptized October 30, 1735. Married George Mercer of Marlboro.

————

The children of GEN. HUGH MERCER 4 (23) and ISABELLA GORDON (24), his wife, were:

1. Anna Gordon Mercer 5. Married Robert Patton of Fredericksburg, Va. In a letter from Mrs. Dunbar, who was Eliza-

beth Gregory Thornton, to her sister, Mrs.
Frances Thornton of Fall Hill, *née* Miss
Innes, daughter of Judge Innes of Kentucky, she wrote of this marriage: "But if
I go on so fast I will not have time to tell
you about Miss Ann Mercer's wedding.
Well, Polly and myself were drawn forth in
our best airs on the occasion, last Thursday
was a week, and saw Miss M. give her hand
to the delighted Mr. Patton. You may be
sure she looked infinitely lovely; her dress
was white satin and muslin; her necklace,
earrings and bracelets were very brilliant."

2. John Mercer 5. Born 1772. Died
September 30, 1817.

3. William Mercer 5. Died unmarried.
He was deaf and dumb.

4. George Weedon Mercer 5. Died unmarried.

5. Hugh Tenant Weedon Mercer 5. He
was a child in arms at his father's death.
He was educated at the expense of the nation by act of Congress of 1793. He married Louisa Griffin 5, daughter of Judge
Cyrus Griffin by Lady Christina Stuart.

Col. Hugh Mercer 5 (31) was born in
Fredericksburg, August 4, 1776, died at
the "Sentry Box," Fredericksburg, December 1, 1853. His wife, Louisa Griffin

Mercer 5 (32), died December 28, 1859, aged 80 years. These dates are taken from the tombs in the Masonic Cemetery in Fredericksburg.

THE DESCENDANTS OF ROBERT PATTON AND ANNE GORDON MERCER

ROBERT PATTON 5 (27) was a Scotchman. He emigrated to Virginia some time before the Revolutionary War, settled in Fredericksburg, Va., and there married ANNE GORDON MERCER 5 (26), only daughter of GEN. HUGH MERCER 4 (23), about 1793, but prior to November 25th of that year *vide* will of General Weedon.

The children of Robert Patton and Anne Gordon Mercer 5 (26), his wife, were:

1. Robert Patton 6, a distinguished lawyer of Fredericksburg, Va. President of Farmers' Bank. He died, unmarried, at about the age of thirty-five, in 1830, in Spottsylvania County, Va.

2. Hugh Mercer Patton 6. Died unmarried in 1846.

3. John Mercer Patton 6. Born August 10, 1797. Died October 29, 1858. He was for many years the acknowledged leader of the Richmond Bar, a Representative in Congress from Virginia, and for a short

time Governor of the State of Virginia. He
married on January 8, 1824, Margaret
French Williams 6, by whom he had twelve
children.

4. Eleanor Anne Patton 6. Born ——,
1805. Died June 24, 1890. She married on
March 24, 1825, John James Chew 6. Born
——, 1806. He was Clerk of Courts of
Fredericksburg. Died January 23, 1870,
at Fredericksburg, Va., and had six
children.

5. William Fairlie Patton 6. Born
——. Died ——. He married Harriet
Shepherd Buck 6 and had five children by
her.

6. Margaretta L. Patton 6. Born ——,
1810. Died July 2, 1852. She married, on
April 18, 1835, John Minor Herndon 6.
Born May 14, 1808. Died September 19,
1871, and had three daughters.

Robert Patton 5 (27). Died in 1827 or
1828.

See report of Commissioner Thomas D.
Ranson in suit of Patton's Exec. against
Patton's creditors in Circuit Court of Au-
gusta County, Va., of 1871.

THE DESCENDANTS OF ROBERT PATTON AND
ANNE GORDON MERCER

The children of the HONOURABLE JOHN
MERCER PATTON 6 (35) and MARGARET
FRENCH WILLIAMS 6 (36), his wife, were:

1. Robert Patton 7. Born October 10,
1824. Died, unmarried, June 13, 1876.

2. John Mercer Patton 7. Born May 9,
1826. He married first on November 11,
1858, Sallie Lindsay Taylor 7, daughter of
Alex. Taylor of Orange, Va. She died on
December 28, 1872. He married, second,
Lucy Agnes Crump, born April 29, 1846,
by whom he had two children, both girls.
Died on October 9, 1878.

3. Isaac Williams Patton 7. Born February 4, 1828. Died February —, 1890.
He married Fanny Elizabeth Merritt 7 on
February 29, 1855. He held many prominent positions in New Orleans. There were
three sons by this marriage.

4. Lucy Anne Patton 7. Born November 7, 1829. Died October 31, 1831.

5. Hugh Philip Patton 7. Born July 7,
1831. Died April 2, 1832.

6. George Smith Patton 7. Born June
26, 1833. Died September —, 1864. He
settled as a lawyer in West Virginia, volun-
teered in the late war between the States,
became a Colonel and was killed at the

battle of Winchester, near the close of the war. He married Susan Glassell 7, November 8, 1855, and had by her four children. Mrs. Patton afterwards was married to Col. George Hugh Smith of Los Angeles, Cal. He was the son of the Rev. George Archibald Smith of Alexandria, who married Ophelia Williams, sister of Margaret French Williams. There were two children by this second marriage: a girl, Anne Patton Smith, who married Hancock Banning of Los Angeles; and a boy, who died, full of promise, quite young.

7. Waller Tazewell Patton 7. Born July 15, 1835. Died July 21, 1863. He was Colonel in the Southern Army and Senator in the Virginia Legislature. He was mortally wounded at the Battle of Gettysburg, July 3, 1863, and died a few days later, unmarried.

8. Mary Mercer Patton 7. Born April 14, 1837. Died August 29, 1841.

9. Eliza Williams Patton 7. Born February 22, 1839. Married on November 15, 1860, to John Gilmer 6, born January 13, 1826, of Chatham, Va. He died March 12, 1894. They had several children.

10. Hugh Mercer Patton 7. Born April 6, 1841. Married Fannie Bull 7, of Orange,

Va., on October 19, 1870. They had several children.

11. James French Patton 7. Born September 19, 1843. Died while Judge of the Supreme Court of West Virginia, at Wheeling, on March 30, 1882. He married on April 6, 1869, Melinda Caperton 7, daughter of Senator Caperton of Union, Monroe County, Va., and had by her two children.

12. William Macfarland Patton 7. Born August 22, 1845. Died May 19, 1905. He studied engineering, and while Professor of Civil and Military Engineering at the Virginia Military Institute, he married Miss Annie Jordon on January 7, 1875, by whom he had several children, all girls. She afterwards married Judge Bingham of the Supreme Court of District of Columbia.

The children of Col. Jno. Mercer Patton 7 (44) and Sally Lindsay Taylor 7 (45), his first wife, were:

1. Jno. Mercer Patton, Junior, 8. Born August 30, 1859. He married on June 28, 1890, Julia Mattern. They had two children:

a. Catherine 8. Born April, 1891.

b. Jno. Mercer Patton (9), Jr. Born April, 1892.

2. Alexander Taylor Patton 8. Born April 19, 1861. He married Miss Beatrice Chandler of San Francisco in June, 1901. Died November, 1904. No issue.

3. Sadie Lindsay Patton 8. Born February 7, 1863. She married on September 19, 1888, Capt. Arthur Jno. Hutchinson 8 (R. A.), who was born August 31, 1846. Their children are:

a. Mary Lindsay Hutchinson 9. Born August 4, 1890.

b. William Nelson Lindsay Hutchinson 9. Born December 7, 1892.

c. Arthur John Lindsay Hutchinson 9. Born August 18, 1896.

4. George Tazewell Patton 8. Born December 25, 1864. He was married on December 10, 1890, to Virginia (Jennie) King Pemberton 8. Born February 1, 1864. They have children:

a. Mary Pemberton Patton (9). Born December 3, 1893.

b. William Rives Patton (9). Born May 5, 1898.

c. George Tazewell Patton (9). Born January 31, 1902.

5. James Lindsay Patton 8. Born November 20, 1866. Married June 28, 1890, to Fanny Kean Leake 8, daughter of Judge W. J. Leake of Ashland, Va., and later of

Richmond, Va. He was a minister of the Episcopal Church and Missionary to Japan. Their children are:

1. John Mercer Patton (9), Jr. Born June 7, 1891. Died July 1, 1892.

2. Sadie Patton 9. Born July 5, 1893.

3. Martha Callis Patton 9. Born October 5, 1896.

4. James Lindsay Patton 9. Born December 13, 1900.

5. William Josiah Leake Patton 9. Born July 28, 1902.

6. Fanny Leake Patton 9. Born March 10, 1905.

7. Robert Williams Patton 8. Born February 18, 1869. Married on January 1, 1900, Janie Slaughter Stringfellow. Born August 15, 1876, daughter of Rev. Frank Stringfellow of Raccoon Ford, Va., and Emma Francis Green, born 1843, of Alexandria, Va. Issue:

Alice Lee Patton 9. Born July 25, 1901, near the Meadows in Albermarle County, Va.

8. William Rives Patton 8. Born April 3, 1871. Died May 29, 1897. Unmarried.

9. Alfred Slaughter Patton 8. Born October, 1872. Died July 28, 1873.

THE DESCENDANTS OF ANNE GORDON MERCER
AND ROBERT PATTON.

The children of Col. Jno. M. Patton (44) and Lucy Agnes Crump, his second wife, are:

9. Susan French Patton 8. Born September 11, 1884.

10. Agnes Parke Patton 8. Born February 19, 1887.

The children of Col. Isaac Williams Patton 7 (46) and Fanny E. Merritt 7 (47) were:

1. William Thomas Patton. Born March 18, 1856. Died July 4, 1896.

2. Mary Mercer Patton. Born March 9, 1861. Died August —, 1864.

3. George Tazewell Patton. Born November 14, 1864.

4. Mercer Williams Patton. Born October 26, 1867. Married.

THE DESCENDANTS OF ROBERT PATTON AND
ANNE GORDON MERCER

The children of George Smith Patton 7 (50) and his wife, Susan Thornton Glassell 7 (51), were:

George Smith Patton. He married Ruth

Wilson of California. They have two children.

2. Ellen Thornton Patton. She married Tom Brown, Esq., of Los Angeles, Cal. He died about 1895. They have three children.

3. Andrew Glassell Patton.

4. Susan Glassell Patton. Married 1904.

THE DESCENDANTS OF ROBERT PATTON AND HIS WIFE, ANNE GORDON MERCER

The children of Eliza Williams Patton 7 (54) and John Gilmer 7 (55), her husband, were:

1. John Patton Gilmer. Born September 9, 1861. Married on October 16, 1895, to Lucy Dabney Walker. Born October 10, 1872. They have one child.

2. William Wirt Gilmer. Born May 21, 1863. Unmarried.

3. Tazewell Gilmer. Born March 30, 1865.

4. Mary Ridgeway Gilmer. Born August 9, 1866.

5. Francis Walker Gilmer. Born May 23, 1868. Died November 7, 1879.

6. Mercer Williams Gilmer. Born December 30, 1869. Unmarried.

7. James Carrington Gilmer. Born December 7, 1871.

8. Lindsay Gilmer. Born July 7, 1873.
9. Isabel Breckinridge Gilmer. Born December 26, 1879.

THE DESCENDANTS OF ROBERT PATTON AND
ANNE GORDON MERCER

The children of Hugh Mercer Patton 7 (56) and Frances Dade Bull 7 (57) were:
1. Marguerita French Patton 8. Born September 22, 1871. She married on June 9, 1895, George Harmer Gilmer 8, born December 19, 1864, son of Judge George Henry Gilmer of Chatham, Va. They live in Lynchburg, Va. Issue:
   a. Helen Mercer Gilmer 9. Born January 8, 1896.
   b. Rita Carrington Gilmer. Born July 10, 1899.
2. Sally Lindsay Patton. Born September 15, 1872. Died ——.
3. Frances Payton Patton. Born May 4, 1876.
4. John Mercer Patton. Born January 11, 1878.
5. Marie Louise Patton. Died in infancy.
6. Mabel Blair Patton. Born June 27, 1881.

7. Helen Lee Patton. Born October —, 1882.

8. Marcus Dade Patton. Died in infancy.

9. Clayton Lorenzo Patton. Born August 11, 1892. Died in infancy.

———

THE DESCENDANTS OF ROBERT PATTON AND ANNE GORDON MERCER

James French Patton 7 (58). Married Melinda Caperton (59) and had issue:

1. Harriet Echols Patton. Born August 25, 1870. Married 1903.

2. Allen Gilmer Patton. Born December 1, 1871. Married 1903.

———

William Macfarland Patton 7 (66). Married Annie Jordon 7 (61) and had issue:

1. Sallie Taylor Patton. Born April 26, 1877. Married on August 28, 1905, at Blacksburg, Va., Prof. ——.

2. Margaret French Patton. Born August 13, 1878.

3. Virginia Mercer Patton. Born September 21, 1880.

4. Nannie Maria Patton. Born July 6, 1882.

5. Agnes Lee Patton. Born September 30, 1884.

6. Lucy Williams Patton. Born December 20, 1886.

7. Elizabeth Jordan Patton. Born January 1, 1876. Died July 13, 1876.

THE DESCENDANTS OF ROBERT PATTON AND ANNE GORDON MERCER

The Chew Family

Eleanor Anne Patton 6 (37). Married John James Chew 6 (38) of Fredericksburg, Va., who was for many years a Clerk of the Courts of Fredericksburg, and had issue as follows:

1. Anne Mercer Chew 7. Born February 26, 1826. Died May 13, 1896. She married, on October 14, 1851, Frank Thornton Forbes. Born January 11, 1826, and died December, 1905, and had issue as follows:

The Forbes Family

a. John James Forbes 8. Born September —, 1852. Died May —, 1855.

b. Sallie Innes Forbes 8. Born August 17, 1854.

c. James Fitzgerald Forbes 8. Born July 14, 1856.

d. Eliza French Forbes 8. Born September 19, 1858.

e. Ellen Patton Forbes 8. Born November 25, 1860. Married Dr. William Wayne Owens of Savannah, Ga., on ——. Issue: William Duncan Owens 9. Born June 22, 1894.

f. Anne Mercer Forbes 8. Born February 4, 1864.

The Chew Family.

Robert Stanard Chew, born October 3, 1828. Died August 17, 1886. Unmarried. Succeeded his father as Clerk of the Courts of Fredericksburg, graduated in medicine, and was Colonel of the 30th Virginia Regiment, C. S. A.

3. Ellen Patton Chew. Born September 17, 1837. Died May 22, 1896. Unmarried.

4. Hugh Patton Chew 7. Born September ——. Died January 30, 1873. He married Bessie Bainbridge 7 on ——, and had three children:

a. Eleanor Patton Chew 8. Born November 13, 1868.

b. John James Chew 8. Born January 22, 1871.

c. Bessie Mason Bainbridge Chew 8.
Born August —, 1873. Died ——.

Mrs. Bessie Bainbridge Chew was married on ——, 18—, to William M. Grafton,
and now resides (May, 1899) at Sewickley,
near Pittsburgh, Pa.

The Crutchfield Family

5. Elizabeth French Chew 7. Born
June 13, 1843.

She married, on January 13, 1865, Edgar
Crutchfield (born March 1, 1840) of Fredericksburg, Va., and had issue:

a. Eleanor Patton Crutchfield 8. Born
May 6, 1866.

She married, on November, —, 1892,
Clement Read Carrington 8, born July 25,
1854, and died ——, and had issue:

1. Abram Cabell Carrington 9. Born
January 26, 1894.

2. Elizabeth Crutchfield Carrington 9.
Born June 30, 1896.

b. Stapleton Crutchfield 8. Born August 24, 1868. Died ——.

He married on September 12, 1893, Mary
Lee Van House, born December 12, 1873,
and had issue by her:

1. Elizabeth Mercer Crutchfield 9. Born
March 18, 1895. Died July 7, 1896.

2. Joy Mantlebert Crutchfield 9. Born December 23, 1896.

c. Susan Gatewood Crutchfield 8. Born December 23, 1870.

Married on October 24, 1895, to Daniel Shriver Russell 8, and had issue:

1. Elizabeth Mantlebert Russell 9. Born August 14, 1896.

2. Eleanor Blain Russell 9. Born October 26, 1898.

———

d. Anne Minor Crutchfield 8. Born February 14, 18—. Died May 22, 1898.

e. Margaretta Taylor Crutchfield 8. Born November 7, 1876.

f. Elizabeth French Crutchfield 8. Born February 3, 1879.

Married Mr. John Minor Gatewood of Boston, June 1, 1905.

g. Mercer Forbes Crutchfield 8. Born August 15, 1881.

———

6. Margaretta Herndon Chew 7. Born April, 1846.

She married, on January 28, 1873, Arthur Taylor (born October 13, 1844) of Fredericksburg, Va. They have issue as follows:

a. Robert Chew Taylor 8. Born October 7, 1879.

b. Fanny Mackall Taylor 8. Born October 4, 1881.

c. Margaretta Mercer Taylor 8. Born April 15, 1885.

The children of William Fairlie Patton 6 (39) and Harriet Shepherd Buck 6 (40) were:

1. Anthony Patton 7. Born ———. Died January 21, 1905.

He married Virginia Bernard Coakley on ———, 18—. No issue.

2. Mary Patton 7, twin of the above. Born ———. Died ———.

She married Richard Henry Catlett 7, born ———, of Staunton, Va. They have three children.

3. William Fairlie Patton 7. Died ———.

4. ———. Died in infancy.

5. Anne Gordon Patton 7. Born ———.

She married, on ———, 18—, Gen. Jno. Rogers Cooke. Born June 10, 1833. Died April 10, 1891, and had eleven children.

6. Fairlie Preston Patton 7. Born March 10, 1851.

He married Winnie T. Branham (born April 18, 1853) on April 18, 1875. They have five children.

The children of Mary Patton 7 (163) and Richard Henry Catlett 7 (164) are:

1. Charles Catlett. Born August 18, 1865.

He married, on November 6, 1890, Elizabeth Marye Hunton, daughter of James Innis Hunton of Warrenton, Va., and had issue by her as follows:

a. Lucy Hunton Catlett. Born September 26, 1891.

b. Richard Henry Catlett. Born October 19, 1892.

c. Elizabeth McNemara Catlett. Born June 22, 1895.

2. Richard Henry Catlett. Born November 27, 1868.

3. William Fairlie Catlett. Born August 8, 1871. Died November —, 1872.

The Cooke Branch

The children of Anne Gordon Patton 7 (167) and Gen. Jno. Rogers Cooke 7 (168) were:

1. Jno. Rogers Cooke (8), Jr. Born March 29, 1865.

2. Fairlie Patton Cooke 8. Born May 2, 1867.
Married October 26, 1904, to Miss Mary Edmonia Rogers of Richmond, Va.

3. Ellen Mercer Cooke 8. Born ——.
She married, on November 14, 1895, Austin Brockenbrough 8. Born April 18, 1862, and had issue:

a. Austin Brockenbrough. Born July 6, 1899.

b. Anne Gordon Brockenbrough. Born April 27, 1903.

4. Philip St. Geo. Cooke 8. Born November 3, 1871.

5. Esten Cooke 8. Born March 10, 1873. Died ——, 1873.

6. Wilt Cooke 8. Born March 10, 1873. Died ——, 1873.

7. Rachel Cooke 8. Born June 16, 1874.

8. Harriet Shepherd Cooke 8. Born August 10, 1876. Married, on March 27, 1900, to Mr. William Jefferson Wallace. Born ——, 18—. Issue: Virginia Gordon Wallace. Born March 12, 1903.

9. Nanny Gordon Cooke 8. Born October 5, 1878. Married, on October 24, 1905, Stafford A. Parker, of Richmond, Va.

10. Stuart Cooke 8. Born December 8, 1879. Married, on January 22, 1903, to

Miss Martha Ann Lundy (born July 18,
——) of Richmond, Va.

———

The children of Fairlie Preston Patton 7
(169) and Winnie T. Branham 7 (170) are:
1. Fairlie Clifton Patton. Born December 4, 1876.
2. Sterling Hume Patton. Born December 19, 1878. Died December 28, 1878.
3. Robert Antony Patton. Born December 13, 1879.
4. Mary Alice Patton. Born May 8, 1884.
5. Eugenie Virginia Patton. Born April 24, 1886.
6. William Henry Patton. Born December 22, 1887.
7. John Mercer Patton. Born February 9, 1891.
8. Winnie Baidie Patton. August 6, 1893.
9. Hugh Peyton Patton. October 26, 1895.

The Herndon Family

The children of Margaretta Patton 6
(41) and John Minor Herndon 6 (41) were:
1. Ellen Mercer Herndon 7. Born April 29, 1836. Died January 29, 1888.

2. Nanny Gordon Herndon 7. Born ——, 1838. Died August 1, 1862.

3. Elizabeth Fairlie Herndon 7. Born ——, 1841. Died January 3, 1892.

She married, on ——, 18—, Seth Barton French 7 (born October 5, ——), who is a prominent financier in the city of New York. They had three children:

a. Margaretta Patton French 8. Born July 25, 1857. Died November 30, 1878.

b. John Herndon French. Born August 4, 1859.

He married, on November 14, 1888, Sarah Ann Spies Cockrane 8 (born February 18, 1865), by whom he has children:

1. Seth Barton French, Jr. Born August 17, 1889.

2. Hilah Cockrane French. Born January 28, 1891.

3. Ellen Mercer French. Born March 8, 1896.

4. John Herndon French, Jr. Born February 26, 1898.

c. George Barton French 8. Born February 12, 1864.

Married Adela Lesher on April 29, 1886. No issue.

He next married Miss —— of Denver.

d. Nannie Gordon French 8. Born March 25, 1866.

She married, on April 21, 1885, Charles Steele 8 (born May 5, 1857), who is a member of the firm of J. P. Morgan & Co., bankers, New York City. They have children:

a. Eleanor Herndon Steele 8. Born July 12, 1891.

b. Nancy Gordon Steele 9. Born October 11, 1894.

c. Catheryn Nevitt Steele. Born March 1, 1896.

THE DESCENDANTS OF COL. HUGH MERCER
AND LOUISA GRIFFIN

The children of Col. Hugh Mercer 5 (31) of the "Sentry Box," Fredericksburg, Va., and Louisa Griffin 5 (32), his wife, were:

1. Hugh Weedon Mercer 6. Born November 27, 1808. Died June 9, 1877. He settled in Savannah, Ga. Married, first, Mary Stiles Anderson 6 (born September 17, 1812; died February 3, 1855) of Savannah, Ga., on February 5, 1834, and had by her six children. He married, second, Mrs. George A. Cuyler 6 (*née* Steenberger) of Virginia, and had one child, a daughter.

He was Major-General in the Confederacy, and died at Baden-Baden, Germany.

2. George Weedon Mercer 6. Born

January 3, 1816. Died September 9, 1858, unmarried.

3. Julia Weedon Mercer 6. Born ——. Died December 10, 1883.

She married, on May 12, 1825, Dr. Robert Page Waller 6 (born ——; died July 21, 1872) of Williamsburg, Va., and had issue.

4. John Cyrus Mercer 6. Born at Fredericksburg, May 12, 1810. Died March 26, 1884. He practiced medicine in Williamsburg, Va.; was appointed Surgeon in the U. S. Navy; resigned; appointed Surgeon in the Confederate States Navy; with the Marine Hospital, Norfolk.

He married Catherine Waller 6, died May 24, 1892, daughter of Dr. Robert Page Waller, and had issue.

5. Louisa Mercer 6. She married Rev. Dr. John Leyburn 6, a Presbyterian minister. Born ——. Died ——. No issue.

Miss Julia Weedon Mercer was the second wife of Dr. R. P. Waller, his first wife being Eliza Corbin Griffin.

The children of Gen. Hugh Weedon Mercer 6 (211) and Mary Stiles Anderson 6 (212), his first wife, are:

1. George Anderson Mercer 7. Born February 9, 1835.

He married, on October 23, 1861, Nanny Maury Herndon 7 (died June 16, 1885) of

Fredericksburg, Va., daughter of Dr. Brodie Herndon, and by her had issue:

1. Nannie Herndon Mercer 8. Born January 8, 1866.

She married, on April 24, 1889, Joseph Muir Lang 8 (born February 4, 1861) and has issue:

a. George Mercer Lang. Born July 13, 1894.

2. George Anderson Mercer. Born March 2, 1868.

He married, on April 19, 1892, Mary Walter 8 of Savannah, Ga. (born October 8, 1872), and has issue:

a. George Anderson Mercer. Born February 7, 1893.

b. George Walter Mercer. Born April 20, 1897.

3. Lewis Herndon Mercer 8. Born March 4, 1870. Settled in New York.

4. Robert Lee Mecrer 8. Born November 24, 1871.

He married, on October 27, 1896, Katherine Mackay Stiles 8 of Cartersville, Ga. Born April 29, 1870.

5. Edward Clifford Anderson Mercer 8. Born November 13, 1873.

He married, on June 8, 1898, Josephine Freeland 8 of Charleston, S. C. Born March 4, 1875.

6. Hugh Weedon Mercer 8. Died in infancy, February 3, 1871. Born August 25, 1863.

7. Brodie Herndon Mercer 8. Born ——, 1876. Died in infancy, June 13, 1878.

3. Hugh Weedon Mercer 7. Born March 3, 1846. Died June 7, 1847.

2. William Gordon Mercer 7. Born May 26, 1843. Died November 26, 1844.

4. Robert Lee Mercer 7. Born July 10, 1848.

5. Mary Stuart Mercer 7. Born January 12, 1842.

She married, on February 5, 1863, General Henry Harrison Walker of Sussex County, Va. (born October 15, 1833), and has issue. General Walker's father was John Harrison Walker of Sussex County, Va., and his mother was Marie Louise Cargill, also of Sussex County. They had ten children, of whom General Walker was second child.

6. Georgia Anderson Mercer 7. Born September 6, 1851. Died December 5, 1878.

She married, on January 15, 1874, Robert Apthorp Boit of Boston, Mass. (Born April 29, 1846.) She died at the birth of her second child, leaving two daughters.

1. Mary Anderson Mercer 8. Born September 5, 1877.

2. Georgia Mercer 8. Born November 25, 1875.

The child of Gen. Hugh Weedon Mercer 6 (211) and Mrs. George A. Cuyler 6 (*née* Bessie Steenberger) (213), his second wife, is:

1. Alice.

The children of Gen. Henry H. Walker 7 (251) and Mary Mercer 7 (250) are:

1. Mary Mercer Walker 8. Born May 29, 1864.

She married, on September 17, 1890, George Evelyn Harrison 8 of Brandon-on-the-James-River, Va.

2. Louise Cargill Walker 8. Born September 25, 1869.

3. Henry Harrison Walker 8. Born January 11, 1872.

4. Hugh Mercer Walker 8. Born April 17, 1876.

5. Alice Stuart Walker 8. Born November 24, 1877.

She married, on January 7, 1899, Edwin A. Stevens Lewis of Castle Point, Hoboken, N. J.

The children of Dr. Robert Page Waller 6 (216) and Julia Weedon Mercer 6 (215) were:

1. Hugh Mercer Waller 7. Born December, 1829. Died May 30, 1896.

2. Laura Page Waller 7. Born July 31, 1828.

She married, on October 15, 1846, Dr. William Sylvanus Morris 7 of Lynchburg, Va. (born March 17, 1821; died December 20, 1893), and had issue:

3. Louisa Mercer Waller 7. Born February 7, 1826. Died October 30, 1856. She married Captain J. B. Cosnahan of South Carolina 7 (born 1821, died 1862) on ——, 1843, and had issue:

4. Julia Weedon Waller 7. Born November 23, 1836. Died October 30, 1860.

5. Isabella Stuart 7. Born 1833. Died May 15, 1855.

Kate Page Waller 7. Born November 15, 1840.

She married, on July 3, 1861, Charles Scott Langhorne 7 (born January 23, 1836; died March 31, 1896).

(Issue: page 95 of Notebook of Mercer Family.)

————

The children of Dr. William Sylvanus Morris 7 (280) and Page Waller 7 (279) were:

1. Mary Mercer Morris. Born ——.
She married, on ——, Mr. Nowlin of Lynchburg.

2. Charles Morris.

3. Robert Page Waller Morris. He married.

Judge of United States District Court of Minnesota, appointed by President Roosevelt, and late Member of Congress from Minnesota.

4. John Speed Morris 8.

He married, on February 19, 1882, Pattie Cary Kean 8 (born April 11, 1858) and had issue:

a. Robert Morris 9. Born ——, 1883.

b. Mary Randolph Morris 9.

c. Page Waller Morris 9. Born July 1, 1896.

d. William Sylvanus Morris 9. Born May 6, 1888.

5. Lou Belle Morris 8.

She married, first, Mr. Langhorne of Lynchburg, and had issue:

1. Sallie.

2. Bessie.

She married, second, on ——, Robert Stanard 8, and left issue:

1. Virginia. Born ——.

2. ——. Born ——.

The children of J. B. Cosnahan 8 (282) and Louisa Mercer Waller 8 (281) are:

1. Roberta Ould Cosnahan 9. Born April 29, 1844.

She married, on December 25, 1871, Charles Camm 9, born April 18, 1844, and had issue living:

Florence Waller Camm. Born March 9, 1874.

Edward Camm. Born February 28, 1876.

Louise Page. Born September 2, 1879.

3. Mary Mercer Cosnahan 9. Born October 5, 1850.

She married, on December 22, 1869, Prof. Thomas Jeffres Stubbs 9 of William and Mary College (born September 14, 1841), and had issue living:

a. Annie Waller Carter Stubbs 10. Born January 7, 1872.

b. J. T. Stubbs, Jr., 10. Born December 11, 1879.

c. Lucy Talioferro Conway Stubbs. Born October 11, 1882.

d. Mary Mercer Stubbs. Born June 1, 1885.

———

The children of Dr. John Cyrus Mercer 6 (217) and Mary Catherine Waller 6 (218) were:

1. Robert Page Mercer 7. Died in infancy.

2. Mary Louisa Mercer 7. Born June 12, 1839.

She married, on January 3, 1867, Rev. Daniel Blain 7 (born November 20, 1838) of the West Hanover Presbytery, Va., and had issue:

3. Eliza Christina Mercer 7.

She married, on November 26, 1861, Dr. Beverly St. George Tucker 7 (born ——; died December, 1896), and had issue:

4. Thomas Hugh Mercer 7. Born in 1845. Died 1864. Unmarried. Lieutenant C. S. A.

5. Corbin Waller Mercer 7. Born April 2, 1845.

He married, on November 25, 1885, Fannie Burwell Nelson 7 (born July 16, 1848), daughter of William Nelson of Yorktown, second grandson of Governor Nelson, and had issue:

6. Catherine Stuart Mercer 7. Born at Williamsburg, 1847.

She married, on November 26, 1873, William Stuart Wall (died in Durham, N. C., 1891), and had issue:

7. John Leyburn Mercer 7. Born August 2, 1849.

He married, on March 31, 1875, Jean Sin-

clair Bright 7 (born December 20, 1850),
daughter of Samuel Bright of Williamsburg, and had issue:
8. Blakely Carter Mercer 7. Died in infancy.
9. Robert Page Mercer 7.
He married Sally Tourman 7, and they
have issue:
10. Isabella Stuart Waller Mercer 7.
Born September 29, 1858. She married on
October 18, 1888, Charles McGary 7 (born
November 12, 1858), of Durham, N. C., and
have issue. Charles McGary was son of
Captain P. McGary of the U. S. Navy, and
was born in Buenos Ayres.
2. George Weedon Mercer 7. Born
June 4, 1863.
He married Elizabeth Butterworth 7
(born September 9, 1872) on January 5,
1893, and has issue:

The children of Rev. Daniel Blain 7 (328)
and Mary Louisa Mercer 7 (327) are:
1. Rev. John Mercer Blain 8. Born
April 30, 1869.
He went as a missionary to China and
there married, on August 24, 1897, Claude

Lacy Grier 8 of North Carolina. They have issue:

   a. Daniel Blain 9. Born December 17, 1898.

   b. Mary Grier Blain. Born October 27, 1900.

   c. Margaret Cary Blain. Born October 14, 1903.

   2. Randolph Harrison Blain 8. Born January 12, 1871. Married Jean Throckmorton Forman, August 23, 1899. Issue: (1) Mary Louise. Born August 14, 1900, at Coresville, Va. (2) Stanton Forman. Born in Louisville, Ky., July 22, 1902.

   3. Samuel Stuart Blain 8. Born October 18, 1872.

   4. Hugh Mercer Blain 8. Born December 26, 1874. Married, at Waynesboro, Va., Mary Moore Winston, June 26, 1901. Issue: (1) Elizabeth Winston. Born November 28, 1902. (2) Hugh Mercer. Born August 14, 1905.

   5. Daniel Blain 8. Son of Rev. Daniel Blain and Mary Louise, his wife, *née* Mercer. Born November 23, 1877. Died October 28, 1879.

   6. Robert Waller Blain 8. Born June 18, 1879.

   7. Cary Randolph Blain 8. Born March 11, 1882.

The children of Dr. Beverly St. G. Tucker 7 (330) and Eliza Christina Mercer 7 (329) are:

1. John Speed Tucker 8.
He married.
2. Dr. Beverly Tucker 8.
He married.
3. Eliza Christina Tucker 8. Born ——.
She married.
4. St. George Tucker 8.
5. Hugh Mercer Tucker 8.
6. Henrietta Elizabeth Tucker 8.

—————

The issue of Corbin Waller Mercer 7 (332) and Hannie Burwell Nelson 7 (333) are:

1. William Nelson Mercer 8. Born September 27, 1888. Died April 2, 1889.
2. Waller Nelson Mercer 8. Born November 3, 1891.

—————

The children of William Lewis Wall 7 (335) and Catherine Stuart Mercer 7 (334) are:

1. Mary Stuart Wall 8. Born December 17, 1875.
She married, on June 1, 1898, William Guthrie 8 (born January 12, 1874).

2. Catherine Mercer Wall 8. Born March 7, 1882.

3. William Lewis Wall, Jr., 8. Born September 21, 1887.

———

The children of John Leyburn Mercer 7 (336) and Jean Sinclair Bright 7 (337) are:

1. Jean Christine Mercer 8. Born December 23, 1875.

2. Mary Waller Mercer 8. Born October 13, 1877.

3. Thomas Hugh Mercer 8. Born November 6, 1879.

4. John Leyburn Mercer 8. Born October 11, 1881. Died July 16, 1882.

———

The issue of Robert Page Mercer 7 (340) and Sally Tourman 7 (341) is:

1. Hugh Mercer 8. Born August 4, 1893. Died October, 1904.

———

The issue of Charles McGary 7 (343) and Isabella Stuart Waller Mercer 7 (342) are:

1. ———. Born September 17, ———. Died before being named.

2. Mary Mercer McGary. Born January 29, 1891.

3. Annie Bell McGary. Born February 20, 1893.

4. Isabel Stuart McGary. Born March 15, 1895.

———

The issue of George Weedon Mercer 7 (344) and Bessie Butterworth 7 (345) is:

1. Linden Waller Mercer 8. Born August 19, 1893. Died June 2, 1896.